Made in Whose Image?

Made in Whose Image?

Genetic Engineering and Christian Ethics

Thomas A. Shannon

Humanity Books

an imprint of Prometheus Books
59 John Glenn Drive, Amherst, New York 14228-2197

#42420708

Published 2000 by Humanity Books, an imprint of Prometheus Books

04 03 02 01 00   5 4 3 2 1

Library of Congress Cataloging-in-Publication Data

Shannon, Thomas A. (Thomas Anthony), 1940–
    Made in whose image? : genetic engineering and Christian ethics / Thomas A.
Shannon.
        p.   cm.
    Includes bibliographical references and index.
    ISBN 1–57392–632–9 (alk. paper)—ISBN 1–57392–631–0 (pbk. : alk. paper)
    1. Genetic engineering—Moral and ethical aspects. 2. Christian ethics.
I. Title.
QH442.S477   ~~1999~~ 2000
174'.25—dc21   99–045066
                                                                                    CIP

Printed in the United States of America on acid-free paper

To our daughter Courtney Marie Shannon who, in addition
to having a vinyl pig of her very own,
now has a book of her very own.

CONTENTS

PREFACE

SINCE THE MID-1980s, many new, exciting, and complex developments have occurred in the field of genetics. While many of the core ethical questions and concerns about genetic engineering remain the same, the geography has shifted considerably and the various frameworks in which these core questions are asked and resolved has become even more complex. Additionally, because these new capacities have the potential for significant cultural and ecological implications, the stakes have become even higher.

This work is informed both by my own research in a variety of philosophical and theological areas and by the opportunities provided to me by the Center for Theology and Natural Sciences at the Graduate Theological Union (GTU) in Berkeley. The center, under the leadership of Professors Ted Peters and Robert Russell, secured a three-year grant sponsored by the Ethics, Legal, and Social Implications Program of the Human Genome Project. I am grateful for the research opportunities that this project provided, as well as for the opportunity to meet biannually with many other researchers who provided one another with some of the most critical and constructive peer review I have ever had the pleasure of receiving. In addition to Ted and Bob, this group included Deborah Blake, R. David Cole, Ronald Cole-Turner, Lindon Eaves, Philip Hefner, Solomon Katz, Karen Lebacqz, and Roger Shinn. Suzanne Holland and Donna MacKenzie, graduate students at GTU, also graciously assisted us in our efforts.

I would like to thank Ruth Smith, my colleague in the Humanities and Arts Department at Worcester Polytechnic Institute, for reading the manuscript and making several helpful comments. Richard Sparks, C.S.P., deserves many thanks for much time and effort to help make this a more coherent and readable book. Our daughter Ashley E. Shannon assisted me in the final preparation of the text, and I thank her for her efforts.

INTRODUCTION

ON 13 MAY 1995, a group of religious leaders, under the sponsorship of Jeremy Rifkin of the Foundation on Economic Trends, issued the "Joint Appeal Against Human and Animal Patenting." The statement opposed the patenting of human embryos, genes cells, and the patenting of animals including those with human genes engineered into their permanent genetic code.[1]

This simple statement is a microcosm of many of the problems and concerns raised about modern genetics and about genetic engineering in particular. First is a claim made about science, scientific capabilities, and the social consequence of those capabilities. Not discussed in this statement is whether or not most or many of the issues mentioned in it are in fact ready to be put into practice. Rather, the statement gives the impression that everything it alludes to is ready for clinical or commercial application. Such is not the case. Second, there is a personal, ethical dimension involved, in that genes must be taken from human individuals. The specter raised here is that the rights of unsuspecting individuals will be violated, as if research has not been guided by the doctrine of informed consent or been monitored by Institutional Review Boards for decades. The third dimension is religious, as eighty religious leaders signed this particular statement. Although the participation of this number of religious leaders is important, such individual participation says nothing about denominational positions on genetic engineering. These may or may not support what the various individuals advocate. Fourth, there is a social dimension, in that Jeremy Rifkin has been a leader in various movements opposing genetic developments and applications, from development of the recombinant DNA (deoxyribonucleic acid) technology in the 1970s to genetically engineered food products in the 1990s. To what extent does he represent anyone, or on what basis does he claim the right to be the spokesperson for the general public? Do his claims reflect public opinion, or is he seeking to shape public opinion? A fifth element is the public issue of what those without particular scientific training or expertise think of contemporary genetics and how they think about it. This is a critical area because many developments in the field are complex and difficult to grasp. And it is frequently difficult to separate basic factual information about developments in genetics from questions of ethics and social policy. Sixth is the question of the accuracy of the larger allegations and specific claims made. The issue here is the degree to which an ideological statement correctly presents information and the degree to which such a presentation is shaded by an organization's own interests. Finally, there is the political dimension: What is the purpose of this statement and what motivates it? These questions are not easy to answer, but the questions of interests and political affiliations are critical ones that must not be overlooked.

Questions such as these are associated with various developments in genetics that are reported in national and international print and electronic media almost daily. Developments in genetics are occurring at an ever-increasing pace, a pace that makes serious reflection on the issues even more difficult. Yet there are important religious, social, political, scientific, and ethical issues at stake. And seldom are any of these important dimensions clearly articulated or examined before the next, even more complicated development or application enters the public discussion.

This book is an attempt both to locate the critical issues under debate and to provide a context in which the ethical questions related to these issues can be addressed. As such the book has three main parts. Part I reviews developments in genetics as applied to agriculture, animals, and humans. The chapters in this section essentially present the complex of developments in genetics since the mid-1980s or so. Here I discuss what is being done presently and what future applications may be. Although I do not analyze all of these issues in the subsequent chapters of the book, I think it is important to note the range of social, economic, legal, and ethical problems implied in each area. Part II presents an overview of representative Catholic and Protestant religious perspectives on several genetic developments. The purpose of this section is to give a sampling of the kinds of issues and conversations that are occurring in these religious communities. Frequently such perspectives are dismissed because they are seen as restrictive and alarmist. However, these traditions do raise perspectives that are often ignored or simply not considered worth pursuing from more secular perspectives. And while areas of concern are noted, several authors also see benefits from genetic engineering. Finally, Part III examines both thematic and specific issues in genetic engineering: the sanctity of life, materialism, freedom, nature, and health and disease. These issues cut through many of those presented in the introductory chapters and provide a grounding for how we might begin to think about the resolution of such specific topics as prenatal diagnosis, gene therapy, genetics and behavior, cloning, and the Human Genome Project. Each of these topics has a very theoretical scientific dimension to it, but each also has some very practical applications that will help shape how we think of ourselves and how we interact with one another. I conclude by offering some methodological perspectives.

I am addressing several problems within modern genetics from a perspective that I am developing from my work in the Catholic tradition and my attempts to rethink elements of that tradition. I do this because there are a number of general religious issues that are implicitly and explicitly raised by the new genetics, most notably, the extent of human dominion over the world and the extent to which we can redesign ourselves. Questions such as these lurk around the edges of many of the major debates about the new genetics. Here they will be made explicit. Also, the Catholic Christian tradition has a history of engaging in issues of scientific debate—sometimes for better, and sometimes for worse. When people think of the Catholic Church and science, most recall that church authorities forced Galileo to recant his position on the earth's revolution around the sun, but most also forget that it was the work of Gregor J. Mendel, an Augustinian monk and priest, that laid the foundation for modern genetics. While the record is mixed, some of its traditions can serve us well in examining new questions. For example, Catholicism has a rich theology of the value and goodness of creation, which can help orient us with a certain measure of respect for the genetic material with which we work. This theology appreciates humans as weakened through sin but also as capable of acts of altruism and creativity. This in turn suggests an attitude of watchfulness but not of condemnation as we progress into new areas of research. Catholicism also has an appreciation of the powers of human reason and the capacity to search out the truth. This grounds a basic respect for the project of the sciences, as well as for scientists themselves. Finally, Catholicism has a long history of reflecting on problems in medicine and the sciences. While the vast majority of this history obviously does not contain anything directly related to most of the problems with which this book deals, there is nonetheless a tradition of taking such issues seriously, reflecting on them carefully in light of various beliefs and values and within a methodology. This centuries-old practice of addressing the problems of the day should at least inspire us to respond similarly. And although a tradition cannot and does not provide us with answers to all questions, it does provide points of departure and possibly analogous situations with which to begin our analysis.

I also locate some of my analysis within the Franciscan tradition. In recent years I have been doing work on the Franciscan medieval theologian St. Bonaventure, particularly his theory of human dignity, and on the late-medieval Franciscan philosopher John Duns Scotus, specifically his ethical method. This tradition was part of my own educational development as an undergraduate student, and continuing interest in it has led me to pursue various themes. Furthermore, particularly in terms of my work on Scotus, I have found ideas and ethical perspectives that I think are very useful for addressing some of today's issues. I want to make it very clear that I am neither taking refuge in nostalgia for the Middle Ages nor trying to impose a type of historical Procrustean bed on contemporary issues. Rather, what I have gained from these historical studies is a way of thinking about problems and an appreciation of an ethical methodology. I find Scotus's sensitivity to intentions and circumstances very helpful, thus I have found here a perspective that I can carry with me as I engage in the analysis of contemporary issues in genetics.

Moreover, by addressing questions about genetics from a religious perspective, concerns other than those raised by traditional philosophical perspectives, such as autonomy and risk-benefit analysis and various forms of consequentialist analysis, can be highlighted. While the analysis presented here incorporates such traditional ways of addressing the new genetics, it also widens the scope of vision and analysis. Therefore the effort herein should be seen as complementary, not contradictory, to these philosophical orientations.

I use a religious perspective, particularly the Franciscan tradition, to look at some of the issues in the new genetics from a different angle and to raise some new questions. Thus, later in the book, I will examine themes such as the value of life, human dignity, freedom, individuality, and the theology of nature. These themes establish a context within which the specific practices and problems presented in the introductory chapters of this book can be examined. My efforts are as yet incomplete but not, I hope, inconclusive. My hope is that by standing within this tradition and critically rethinking elements of it, some approaches can be found to help address some of the myriad of problems that follow from contemporary developments in modern genetics.

Finally, I have chosen to discuss issues of methodology in the last chapter rather than in one of the introductory chapters because I have come to the methodological conclusions made only after observing how I think through problems and reflecting on what resources I have brought to bear on them. Thus the location of the methodological material reflects my own process of resolving problems, though one can read this chapter first or last. I hope that by placing it last, the chapter will provide the reader with an opportunity to reflect thematically on the issues that are considered in this book and to evaluate how I have worked through them.

NOTE

1. Edmund L. Andrews, "Religious Leaders Prepare to Fight Patents on Genes," *New York Times*, 13 May 1995, A1, D35.

Part **1** One

DEVELOPMENTS IN GENETICS

THE PURPOSE OF THE following four chapters is to review recent developments and applications in contemporary genetics. Due to the rapid movement of technologies from plant to animal to human applications, such applications are important to understand primarily because they may show up rather soon on our dinner table or in our bodies. Second, these technologies are going to impact significantly on the ways in which medicine is practiced. The options at our disposal will increase dramatically. Third, enormous resources are being expended on the development of these products. This means that market forces will have an exceptionally significant role in both the development of and the incentives to use these technologies and products.

The examples presented are representative of the capacities the new genetics has given us and the types of questions being raised. After a brief overview of developments in the particular area being discussed, each of the following chapters describes various new genetic technologies or applications and then presents some basic questions these technologies and applications raise. Although not all of these questions will be resolved, it is important to recognize the very existence of these questions and to begin to think about how we will approach and attempt to answer them.

STARTING POINTS

THE BIOLOGICAL SCIENCES ARE going through a process of development not unlike that which occurred in nuclear physics in the 1940s. The move from the discovery of the atom to the development of the first atomic bomb to the development of nuclear reactors for power stations and submarines took only a few short decades. Although the initial developments in genetics occurred over a century ago, the advancements in this field just since the 1980s have progressed at a breathtaking pace. Hardly a day goes by without a new discovery or application. This chapter thus reviews some of these developments to set a context for the issues discussed specifically in Part I but also presented thematically throughout the rest of the book.

One of the most critical breakthroughs in modern biology was the theory of inheritance developed by the Austrian monk Gregor J. Mendel. Published in 1865, Mendel's work nevertheless remained virtually unknown until 1900. Three other biologists—Karl E. Correns (Germany), Hugo De Vires (Holland), and Eric Tschermak von Segsenegg (Austria)—all working independently, replicated Mendel's experiments and brought his work to light. Finally it received the recognition it deserved.[1]

While the selective breeding of plants and animals was not unknown before Mendel, the results of such efforts were neither scientific nor predictable. Mendel's insight was that "discrete units of heredity (which he called *Merkmale* and we call genes) are passed unchanged from generation to generation even though each unit is not necessarily expressed as an observable trait in every generation."[2] Additionally, he proposed that for sexually reproducing organisms, each organism "possesses two such units for each observable trait, one inherited from its male parent and the other from its female parent."[3] This insight gave us the ability to develop statistical laws to predict which traits will appear in a particular generation.

This is the model of inheritance familiar to most of us from our high school and college biology courses. The most frequently presented examples of inherited traits are the color and size of plants, eye color, and various diseases. The Mendelian model of inheritance finds a practical application today in genetic screening and prenatal diagnosis, for there are many diseases such as Tay-Sachs or Huntington's disease that follow quite precisely the rules of this model. Thus if one knows the patient's family history, one can make a prediction of the likelihood of various outcomes or, if such a genetic anomaly presents itself during a pregnancy, one can determine the likelihood of another such occurrence. While such analysis cannot determine if a *particular* fetus will be affected with a particular disease, it can tell the *odds* of such an occurrence. Mendel's discovery laid the basis for what became known as *classical genetics*: the study of "those aspects of genetics that can be studied without reference to the molecular details of genes."[4]

The next major development in genetics is referred to as *molecular genetics* and was made possible by the discovery of the existence of genes on chromosomes. This pointed the way to further refinements of the mechanisms of inheritance. Out of these studies came the recognition that many inherited traits are not the work of single genes, as posited by the Mendelian model. Rather, many genes working in combination produced particular effects. This means that prediction is not as straightforward as was thought by classical geneticists.

Then in 1953, James Watson and Francis Crick made their Nobel Prize–winning discovery of the famous double-helix structure of deoxyribonucleic acid (DNA). This model of the DNA molecule provided the basis for understanding how a gene is constructed, how it replicates itself, and how it codes and transfers information. Two insights followed from Watson and Crick's work. First, DNA is the basic mechanism of biological inheritance; second, information is coded in the sequence of the four base acids of which it is composed: adenine, cytosine, guanine, and thymine. The first letters of the names of these four bases—A, C, G, T—serve as the four letters of the genetic alphabet, and their arrangement in various sequences is the basis for the incredible genetic variety we observe daily.

The next dramatic breakthrough occurred in the late 1960s and reached a crescendo in the mid-1970s. This was the technology of recombinant DNA, or rDNA. Essentially, scientists developed the capacity to remove discrete sections of the DNA molecule with chemical scalpels and to replace them with strands from another DNA molecule. The significance and implications of this technology become startlingly clear when one realizes that the replacement DNA need not come from the same organism into which it is inserted. A rather large and frequently raucous national debate followed, focusing specifically on issues of safety (security of research facilities and the life expectancy of such engineered organisms outside the lab), of patenting (who owned the technologies and who could license their use—and control the profits), and of application (curing disease or creating new life-forms).

As the debate continued, so did two other elements of the controversy. First, technical breakthroughs continued at an incredibly rapid rate. Many of the critical pieces of the genetics puzzle had come together, and there was a knowledge and application explosion. Second, safety issues were taken seriously. The Asilomar Conference held in the mid-1970s was organized by the leading scientists in the rDNA revolution and recommended a pause in research until the basic safety issues could be addressed. A federal oversight committee—the rDNA Committee—was then established to supervise critical safety and ethical issues.

The current chapter in this story is the Human Genome Project (HGP): the mapping of the approximately six billion base pairs of DNA in our forty-six chromosomes. As one can imagine, this is a rather vast project—vast enough to require a projected $3 billion and a fifteen-year completion time. The purpose of the HGP is to develop a map of the location of every gene on each chromosome. This map will provide researchers with sites for particular genes so they can study how each functions both by itself and in relation to other genes. Such a resource will be of extraordinary importance as scientists continue to study the way our genes function and help shape our future.

With these developments in genetics comes a certain nervousness. There is concern about the possibility of environmental harm from genetically engineered plants. Some wonder about long-term implications for human well-being from our use of genetically engineered grains and animals, as well as medications. Still others are worried about the misuse of these technologies in human applications.

Concerns such as these are well founded because we do know that not all side effects of scientific discoveries show up quickly, that what we initially think to be beneficial or useful can turn out to be harmful, and that technical capacities themselves can be applied both harmfully and beneficially. Nonetheless, creativity, inquisitiveness, and a desire for self-understanding at all levels are also significant parts of the human condition. What might tampering with these qualities mean for our sense of self?

Developments in genetics therefore force the emergence of a number of critical questions for us as scientists, as citizens, and as members of an ever more tightly knit world community: Are there limits to our desires? Are there limits to our capacities? Should we do everything we can? How do we evaluate harm and benefit? Is some knowledge too dangerous? Should we trust ourselves with such powerful new knowledge?

What I find interesting is that while much of the new genetic technology and applications are breathtaking, many of the questions they give rise to are perennially challenging ones. In addition to the questions previously presented, we grapple with issues of privacy, confidentiality, autonomy, consent, and identity. The new genetics is putting a sharper edge on these traditional questions because of the significance of the implications not only for humans, but also for other species and the environment; and it is also heightening the sense of urgency with which we need to resolve these questions because of the rate of technological development.

Complicating these dimensions are two particular cultural conditions within which these questions arise. One is that we are in a period of various forms of ethical, cultural, and epistemological relativism. However, we have learned one important and critical lesson from these relativisms: Both the questions we ask and the resolutions they necessitate reflect powerful class, racial, and gender presuppositions. We have learned that context in fact shapes the very questions we raise. Second, we are in a period of an explosion of rights claims, from the right to die to the right to have a child of a particular sex. However, profound issues such as those raised by the new genetics have not, cannot, and will not be resolved by various groups hurling rights claims against one another. Nor will they be resolved by the endless multiplications of rights claims by individuals or groups. At best such a position results in a rights standoff; at worst the language of rights is cheapened and the moral and legal status of rights is destroyed.

Social conflict, while perhaps necessary and always understandable in a pluralistic society such as the United States, may have reached its useful limits. And while the politics of difference has made an important contribution to our culture, what we need now is a politics of communality to help us begin a positive and critical evaluation of the new genetics. This is a rather large order. Recent decades have been characterized by a strong philosophy of individualism, of suspicion, of mistrust, and of fear. Although the sources of such an agenda have not disappeared—nor are they likely to in the near future—we need to move beyond self-interest couched in rights language as the primary variable in social and ethical analysis. Otherwise goods and resources that are common to or serve to benefit the community or nation stand in danger of being destroyed or severely depleted. Moreover, issues of safety and the integrity of the environment may be overrun by individuals or groups whose main motive is a rapid return on investments.

The task of establishing a politics of communality is difficult, but it is made even more so by the complexity of the issues involving genetics and the profound personal and social questions they raise. Yet the technologies and their applications continue to expand, and the problems continue to mount. Necessity, if not old-fashioned self-interest, will force us to come to terms with the problems. The question is, will we do this in a constructive way or will we attempt to finesse the issues?

One part of modern genetics that causes tremendous problems is simply the incredibly rapid pace of development. Announcements of the discovery of the location of a specific gene or a new genetic technology to assist in the mapping project occur almost daily. Two further problems are associated with this. First is the difficulty of just trying to keep up with such technical developments and announcements. Second, and more critical, is thinking through what, if any, social and ethical implications such developments might have. This is difficult because implications may not be obvious at first, and some of the implications may emerge only after the technology is well established. Thus, sounding a cautionary note about the implications of modern genetics is neither an antiscience act nor an instance of crying wolf. It is simply a recognition that technical developments outpace our capacity to think them through carefully.

Developments in modern genetics will also bring a number of benefits to many people. Of most concern—and this is a thematic issue in bioethics— is who the recipients of these benefits will be and what these benefits will cost. For example, most research has focused on diseases caused by a single gene, such as Huntington's disease. Although this disease is devastating, it does not affect a large number of people. Diseases with a single genetic cause are studied because only one gene is involved and such a gene is relatively easy to find. But the discovery of the gene comes at a high cost with benefit to relatively few people.

There is also tension between promise and delivery. Many people feel the HGP has been sold on the basis of providing cures for many, if not most, diseases. While it is clear that there is a genetic component to disease, several other issues are involved. First, most diseases are multigenetic in origin. Therefore, no simple cause will be found. Second, even if a single genetic cause is found, there is still a large gap between this discovery and its subsequent cure. Such a gap increases exponentially when the cause is multigenetic. Honesty and realism in genetic promise making are thus critical if public trust is to be maintained.

The question of risk from genetic applications continues to be a central one. This question has been raised in relation to developments in plant, agricultural, and human genetics, and it is raised with respect to basic research as well as to clinical applications of this research. Part of the problem here is that individuals' perceptions of risk vary dramatically. While some of this variation is due to one's personality traits, some is a function of one's interests and values and one's sense of the priority of genetic research, as well as issues relating to deep ecology such as the status of the environment and the integrity of species. Thus the question of the evaluation of risk is itself embedded in a larger set of difficult social questions.

Ultimately, questions such as these point to the issue of human responsibility, particularly as it relates to the human world, but also as it relates to the plant and animal worlds. Do humans have infinite capacities, or do our powers have limits? Is the future ours to design, or are there built-in structures we must respect? To what extent, if at all, can the new genetics influence evolution? These questions, and others like them, point to the real power that we have obtained through the new genetics. While not all of this power can be actualized at the present time, the potential is there, and its realization may be simply a matter of time rather than one of technical breakthrough. And while it is true that the question of the capacity to redesign ourselves is a significant one in light of the new genetics, the more critical question may be the understanding of human nature that such a capacity gives us. Who we think we are and what we think about that may be more critical than the capacity to actualize such a vision.

Thus the stakes in our debates about genetic engineering are high, perhaps higher than we ever foresaw. The issues are more complex than we realized, and society itself seems more divided than ever on these issues. A critical discussion of these issues needs to be at the center of public attention. Such a discussion will be difficult and divisive, but if we as a society do not engage in it, decisions will be made anyway and applications will continue. The onus of decision making is clearly on us.

NOTES

1. Robert P. Wagner, "Understanding Inheritance: An Understanding of Classical and Molecular Genetics," *Los Alamos Science* 20 (1992): 16.
2. Ibid.
3. Ibid.
4. Ibid., 28.

AGRICULTURE AND THE NEW GENETICS

THE FLAVRSAVR TOMATO DEVELOPED by Calgene has a genetically engineered gene that helps it resist rotting for about ten days longer than the traditional tomato. The advantage is that it can ripen on the vine, instead of being picked early to ensure that it will not rot during shipping. But a campaign against the use of this tomato has been launched. According to one account, "More than twenty-five hundred restaurants nationwide, including '21,' Chez Panisse, and Spago, have said they will not serve Calgene's tomato, and in some restaurant windows one is beginning to see the boycott symbol—a coil of DNA with a red slash through it."[1]

In an interesting demonstration of market penetration, *Self* magazine ran a story on genetically engineered food products.[2] In addition to the FlavrSavr tomato, the article described the tomato developed by the DNA Plant Technology Corporation (DNAP) in New Jersey. This tomato has an added gene from the Arctic flounder to make it frost resistant, yet it is technically not a genetically engineered tomato because the inserted gene is naturally occurring. It just so happens that the gene lives in a type of flounder found in the Arctic Circle.

Some see these new food products as a boon for both producer and consumer. Others call them "Frankenfood," tapping into the rich source of horrors associated with the Frankenstein myth. Regardless of how one feels about them, more of such products are on the way to our markets. Twenty-six companies are working on seventy different foods, ranging from celery without strings to potatoes that absorb less oil when fried to fungus-, virus-, and pest-resistant crops.[3] Calgene has been "able to raise two hundred and ten million dollars over the last decade, a period in which the company has only once made a profit."[4] Since the tomato market, to take one example, is estimated to be $4 billion a year, one can see that the stakes are quite high.

Naturally, the development of foods with either genetically engineered products or added genes from other species has precipitated numerous debates.

9

One involves whether or not a genetically engineered food contains a new substance. If it does, it must be submitted to the Food and Drug Administration (FDA), which will then analyze it, label it, and regulate it. This is a major step in ensuring the safety of such products because both the developer and the FDA conduct safety tests on the products.

What counts as new is an interesting question. The gene that causes the Arctic flounder to resist freezing occurs naturally in this fish, so the innovation of the DNAP tomato is that this gene has been isolated and spliced into the genes of the tomato—neither altered nor changed, just relocated. To respond to the question of newness, which subjects such products to FDA oversight, the FDA has developed a safety assessment program within a regulatory framework to ensure the safety of foods and animal feeds.[5]

Traditionally developed new foods, whether they are developed through breeding of animals or through hybridization of plants of different genera, do not require FDA approval. These different or improved foods have been entering our markets and our bodies for hundreds of years. The FDA can, however, "remove a food from commerce if there is even a 'reasonable possibility' that a substance added by human intervention might be unsafe."[6] Additionally, the FDA can do premarket review and approval of "substances intentionally added to food if there is a question about safety."[7]

The FDA's safety assessment looks at three issues: the host plant, donor organisms, and new substances introduced into the food. The FDA understands the host to be "the plant that is genetically modified and is the recipient of any newly introduced traits. In general, it is a species commonly used as a source of food."[8] Two concerns are any changes in the concentration or availability of nutrients, such as vitamin C, and the increase of toxicants in the host. Second, the donor is understood to be "the source of the new trait."[9] Again the issue here is the possible transfer of a toxicant that could accompany the desired gene. Third is the new food product itself, and the most significant element here is proteins, "the largest group of substances being introduced into food through recombinant DNA techniques."[10] The key question is: "Does the protein have a safe history of use in food, or is it substantially similar to such a food component?"[11] Of concern are proteins that are toxic or that may cause an allergic reaction, or whether a new protein that has not previously been a constituent of food might be allergenic to the population.

The FDA's approach to these issues is to give guidance to manufacturers for testing the products and for identifying "scientific or regulatory issues where developers may need to consult the FDA."[12] If there is a question about the safety of a particular protein, "the degree of testing these new proteins would be commensurate with any safety concern raised by the objective characteristics of the protein."[13] The FDA also recommends that developers test the "'wholesomeness' of foods derived from new plant varieties as a means of ensuring that the food does not contain high levels of unexpected, acutely toxic substances."[14] Finally, the FDA notes that "substances that have a safe history of use in food and substances that are substantially similar to such substances generally would not require extensive premarket safety testing."[15]

The potential environmental impact of such products is another area of concern. For instance, the genetically engineered microbe Ice-Minus, "a strain of bacterium genetically altered so it would no longer produce the protein that causes dew to freeze when temperatures hit between 25 and 30 degrees Fahrenheit,"[16] is to be sprayed on such crops as strawberries and potatoes to crowd out already present bacteria and to give the crop extra protection against frost. The difference between this bacterium and the one occurring in nature is that the former lacks the one gene that allows ice to form on the crop. Another difference is that the genetically altered bacterium would be released on a large scale directly into the environment, which raises questions about the long- and short-term effects of the use of this bacterium. Jeremy Rifkin, an antitechnology activist, has said that "every introduction is a hit-or-miss ecological roulette" because of the lack of data about long-term consequences.[17] Rebecca Goldberg, former chair of the biotechnology program at the Environmental Defense Fund, differentiated the release of these organisms from evolution by arguing that the consequences of a natural mutation could not be compared to those of "putting millions of altered microbes in a new environment in which those organisms will thrive."[18]

A second set of concerns has been identified by the Union of Concerned Scientists in its 1993 report *Perils Amidst the Promise*.[19] First, because of the vast array of new genes from which to draw, this technology "can add more genes with harmful potential than can traditional breeding."[20] Second, "the organisms containing these new gene combinations may be less predictable in their traits and behaviors than those produced by traditional breeding."[21] Third, because the genes being transferred are advantageous to the plants, these plants could "overcome obvious limits on population growth."[22] Finally, "we simply have no experience with the use and behavior of organisms with the novel genetic makeups of transgenics."[23]

A third concern, voiced by Goldberg, is the development of crops that are resistant to herbicides. Ironically, farmers would then use higher levels of herbicides and become even more dependent on chemicals. Additionally, such resistant crops could pollinate related species of weeds that would then become resistant to herbicides as well.[24] This same concern is noted by the Union of Concerned Scientists, which raises the possibility of such a transgenic crop moving "out of the field to disturb unmanaged ecosystems."[25]

A fourth concern is whether transgenic crops could create new viruses and diseases. Richard F. Allison, a plant molecular virologist, and Ann E. Greene, a graduate student, showed that "pieces of virus that have been inserted through genetic engineering can combine with a newly introduced virus to make a new virus," much like the process that occurs in nature.[26] Their concern is that "inserting such viral resistance into plants could lead to new, and perhaps more virulent plant viruses."[27] Yet there is a counter-claim to this fear: "Whatever interactions do occur in mixed infections rarely result in new pathogenic viruses. . . . New viral diseases are usually due to minor variants of already known viruses and not to new viruses of recombinant origin."[28] But what about transgenic plants? While no definitive answer can be given, the combination of conditions under which recombination could result is unlikely to occur. Additionally, critics argue that it is unlikely that the frequency of such recombinations would be higher than that of the naturally occurring ones. Finally, "it is unlikely that any given new virus will be more viable than competing viruses throughout the full infection cycle."[29]

Of particular concern is the impact of these genetically engineered foods on individuals, a concern that extends to both plants and animals. An FDA report notes that "the transfer of proteins from one food source to another might therefore confer on food from the host plant the allergenic properties of food from the donor plant. For example, the introduction of a peanut allergen into corn might make that variety of corn newly allergenic to people ordinarily allergic to peanuts."[30] For people concerned about this issue, the report contains no good news: "At this time, we are unaware of any practical method to predict or assess the potential for new proteins to induce allergenicity."[31] Thus one must revert to a trial-and-error method.

The ecological implications of genetically engineered products are obviously related to the questions of environmental impact noted above, but they are somewhat broader in scope. Of particular significance here is the potential threat transgenic crops might pose to global centers of crop diversity. These areas have traditionally been the source of new genes, and reliance on transgenic crops could reduce the naturally occurring diversity. Although a transgenic crop is technically a new crop, the fear is that it could crowd out naturally occurring mutations that might have future benefits. Additionally, market pressures may force farmers to abandon their traditional crops in favor of the new transgenic plants.[32] A concomitant problem—one that is not caused by transgenic plants but one that could nonetheless intensify their potential problems—is the abandonment or destruction of natural habitats through the expansion of human populations that convert agricultural or forestland to urban areas. Finally, the fact that a transgenic plant might be shown to be safe for use within the United States "cannot take into account all the environmental variables confronted by a crop used in different countries in different parts of the world."[33] Thus national testing is necessary;

yet the countries where centers of diversity are located are "among those least likely to have the resources needed to protect against the risks of the technology."[34]

The promises of bioagriculture come in many forms and with varying degrees of intensity. But the thematic claims are for more diverse and improved foods, foods engineered to reach the consumer in better condition, increased quantities of food products, foods that are more fit for their environment, and crops less reliant on the use of chemicals, particularly fertilizers. Additionally, there is the promise of the development of new plants as types of "biological factories." For example, in 1988 the gene for human interferon was introduced into turnip plants to see if the gene would make the plant resistant to viral infections. Though this did not happen, the "transgenic plants made large amounts of the interferon. And just as important, the protein was biologically active in animals."[35] Work is being done to develop other plant-derived antibodies, with a possible application being use as supplements for infant formulas.[36]

The problems that have been discussed concern a variety of environmental impacts: the safety and quality of the crops and the foods derived from them, biodiversity, and the economic impact of such transgenic crops. The economic impact is twofold: the research and design money invested in bioagriculture by major corporations and the possible marginalization of small farms or herds in light of increased production capabilities.

Even though the FDA does review and regulate a variety of products produced by bioagriculture, there is currently "no comprehensive statute addressing the environmental risks of transgenic organisms. Instead, products and activities of biotechnology are covered under a patchwork of existing statutes."[37] One issue concerning the FDA's role in bioagriculture is the extent to which it will rely on manufacturers to conduct safety reviews. Another is the application of existing regulations to such novel products as transgenic plants. The regulatory issue is a critical one and needs to be addressed more thoroughly. Part of the regulatory debate will be addressed by the Environmental Protection Agency, which is "expected to publish a rule that clarifies which genetically engineered micro-organisms fall under its regulatory purview."[38]

The safety issue is also critical. And its importance is increased by our knowledge that not all problems from new developments show up in the short term. The dilemma is how to evaluate the long-term risk of something—manufactured or not—released into the environment without actually releasing that organism into the environment to monitor the outcome. The critics of the use of transgenic plants and microbes argue that laboratory conditions cannot adequately simulate the natural environment, but no reasonable alternative has been proposed. One solution is simply to prohibit the development of transgenic plants. This solution is unlikely, not only because of the obvious economic interests, but also because the knowledge of the technology is too well established and disseminated to be effectively contained. The more likely scenario is to monitor the research, development, and use of transgenic products as carefully as possible. This is the recommendation of, for example, the Union of Concerned Scientists, which proposes that "the United States should establish a strong federal program to assess and minimize the risks of transgenic crops before they are commercialized."[39] This seems the most prudent route to follow. We know that nothing is 100 percent safe. But we also know that the research thus far has not demonstrated any substantive risks or health problems as a consequence of the use of bioengineered products. However, vigilant monitoring is in order.

For Rifkin, the issue is not safety but a competition between two ways of thinking. One he calls "World's Fair thinking": "Whatever increases productivity is good and will find a market."[40] The other is an "ecologically based stewardship of the world."[41] Rifkin thinks that the movement against bioengineered foods will be so strong that "no genetically engineered product will make it to the supermarket."[42] But Rifkin's bottom-line question is not, "Is the product safe?" He admits, for example, that the Calgene tomato probably is safe. Rather, he asks, "Who needs it?"[43] When all the rhetoric has been exhausted and all the data presented, that question may indeed be the critical one.

NOTES

1. John Seabrook, "Tremors in the Hothouse," *New Yorker*, 15 July 1993, 33.
2. Stuart Ganner, "Future Food," *Self* (March 1993): 152.
3. Ibid., 155.
4. Seabrook, "Tremors in the Hothouse," 33.
5. David A. Kessler, Michael R. Taylor, James H. Maryanski, Eric L. Flamm, and Linda S. Sahl, "The Safety of Foods Developed by Biotechnology," *Science* 256 (26 June 1992): 1747–9, 1832.
6. Ibid., 1747.
7. Ibid., 1748.
8. Ibid.
9. Ibid., 1749.
10. Ibid.
11. Ibid.
12. Ibid., 1747.
13. Ibid., 1832.
14. Ibid.
15. Ibid.
16. Pamela Weintraub, "The Coming of the High-Tech Harvest," *Audubon* (July– August 1992): 97.

17. Quoted in ibid.
18. Quoted in ibid., 98.
19. Union of Concerned Scientists, *Perils Amidst the Promise: Ecological Risks of Transgenic Crops in a Global Market* (Cambridge, MA: Union of Concerned Scientists, 1993).
20. Ibid., 12.
21. Ibid.
22. Ibid.
23. Ibid.
24. Weintraub, "High-Tech Harvest," 98.
25. Union of Concerned Scientists, *Perils Amidst the Promise*, 10.
26. Keith Schneider, "Study Finds Risk in Making Plants Viral Resistant," *New York Times*, 11 March 1994, A16.
27. Ibid.
28. Bryce W. Falk and George Bruening, "Will Transgenic Crops Generate New Viruses and New Diseases?" *Science* 263 (11 March 1994): 1396.
29. Ibid.
30. Kessler et. al, "Safety," 1832.
31. Ibid.
32. Union of Concerned Scientists, *Perils Amidst the Promise*, 71.
33. Ibid., 72.
34. Ibid., 73.
35. Anne Simon Moffat, "High-Tech Plants Promise a Bumper Crop of New Products," *Science* 256 (8 May 1992): 770.
36. Ibid.
37. Union of Concerned Scientists, *Perils Amidst the Promise*, 13.
38. Richard Stone, ed., "EPA to Spell Out Biotech Regs," *Science* 265 (2 September 1994): 1351.
39. Union of Concerned Scientists, *Perils Amidst the Promise*, 75.
40. Quoted in Seabrook, "Tremors in the Hothouse," 39.
41. Quoted in ibid.
42. Quoted in ibid.
43. Quoted in ibid.

Chapter 3

ANIMALS AND THE NEW GENETICS

IT IS IRONIC THAT the transgenic mouse developed by scientists at the leading U.S. university is engineered to get sick. This mouse, designed by Philip Lerder of Harvard Medical School and Timothy Stewart of Genentech, "is highly susceptible to cancer, and is able to play an important role in research into, for example, the detection of carcinogens or the evaluation of potential anti-cancer drugs."[1] Pride gives way to practicality, as well as to the necessities of research!

The development of transgenic animals has been one of the interesting and exciting breakthroughs of the late twentieth century. Traditionally one had to rely on traditional breeding methods to express a new gene, and this process worked only in animals of the same species. Thus in his continual quest to develop even more tender and meatier chickens, Frank Purdue was limited to the natural endowment of the chicken and the vagaries of biological reproduction. The same was true for all other breeders, whether of horses, dogs, cats, or mice.

What is different now is that genetic information from one species can be introduced and expressed in an animal of a different species. Additionally, such genetic modification can be introduced into the germ line and passed on to the animal's offspring.[2] An example of this is the "knockout mouse," which has a particular gene eliminated from or knocked out of all its cells so that the effects of the elimination can be studied. A new twist on this is knocking out a gene "only in certain tissues, after the early critical period when the gene is needed has passed."[3] This distinction is important, for the gene in question may have a significant role in early embryonic development. This technology allows that development to occur but then removes the gene to study the effects of its absence in the normal adult mouse.

In other research, both human and bovine growth hormones have been inserted into pigs to make them grow faster and leaner. Thus far the results have not been satisfactory, either for the pigs or for the developers. The pigs gain weight faster only when also given a high-protein diet. And, though leaner, the sows "never go into estrous and are sterile, possibly because they are so lean that they do not produce hormones normally."[4] Additionally, the pigs experience muscle weakness and are "susceptible to developing arthritis and gastric ulcers, which often prove fatal."[5]

Genzyme Transgenics of Cambridge, Massachusetts, has a herd of 100 goats genetically bred to "produce human therapeutic and diagnostic proteins in their milk."[6] This process is referred to as *gene pharming*, "a fledgling form of biotechnology in which genes that produce desired proteins, such as those to treat cystic fibrosis or cancer, are transferred into the embryos of dairy animals."[7] These proteins are removed from the milk of the animals and used for human therapy.

A social application of this technology could involve hamster genes. The Syrian golden hamster can tolerate proportionately 40 percent more alcohol than a human, while normal hamsters typically cannot tolerate alcohol at all. One could see an interesting underground market for humans for both sets of genes!

New applications are continually being researched. Sheep, pigs, chickens, and cows have had new genetic material, including human genetic material, inserted into them. Such developments have, as expected, given rise to numerous debates. The issues of safety, animal rights, and patents continue to press, both ethically and legally.

On 11 March 1994, the Pure Food Campaign, a project of the Foundation on Economic Trends, sponsored a full-page ad in the *New York Times* that began, "If you're against artificial hormones and antibiotics in your milk— you better act now."[8] This was one of the salvos being fired in a campaign against the use of rBGH, otherwise known as synthetic bovine growth hormone. This synthetic hormone is a genetically engineered copy of the naturally occurring bovine growth hormone and, when injected into cows, increases their milk production, perhaps by as much as 25 percent. The concern raised by the Pure Food Campaign, orchestrated by Jeremy Rifkin, is that this genetically engineered hormone will also show up in a variety of both dairy products, such as milk and cheese, and meat products, such as hamburger made from dairy cattle, and may present health hazards.

One of the early issues raised by the development of transgenic animals was the traditional one of animal rights. For several years now, there has been a developing animal rights movement that focuses on the use of animals in research, particularly in what some consider to be frivolous research such as that done by the cosmetics industry. Other concerns have been the treatment of animals during research procedures, the intentional blinding of animals, the destruction of brain centers, and infecting animals with diseases of interest to humans. Animal rights groups criticize the use of animals as practice models for surgical techniques, as well as the inadequacy of their housing. As a result of these complaints, numerous changes have been made in the housing of animals, committees have been established at research centers to evaluate the use of animals in research, and some research has been discontinued.

The research leading to the development of transgenic animals is being evaluated within this context. But additional concerns are being brought to the fore in response to technical developments. One particular issue the transgenic technology has dramatically forced is the question of the moral value of the integrity of a species. Such concerns emerge from a sense that a species is a stable biological unit with its own integrity. From an environmental perspective, many argue that species ought not to become extinct. Transgenic technologies pose a threat to this position. While not everyone would go so far as to call transgenic technology "biological beastiality,"[9] many are indeed concerned about the integrity of a species and its place and function in the ecosystem. The concern focuses on the intentional merging of genetic information between species in a way that exceeds the capacities of nature operating through evolution.

Professor B. E. Rollin of Colorado State University has identified several problems relating to transgenic animals. The first is the speed with which we can introduce change into animals. This can alter the organism itself, for the particular characteristic one is genetically engineering "may have implications that are unsuspected."[10] Without some oversight of this process, there may be a harmful impact on humans who either eat such animals or use the products derived from them.

The second problem relates to the implications of "the narrowing of the gene pool, the tendency towards genetic uniformity, the emergence of harmful recessives, the loss of hybrid vigor, and, of course, the greater susceptibility of organisms to devastation by pathogens."[11] Rollin does note here that such genetic engineering could have the opposite effect, but the concerns he raises are long-standing. We do know that even traditional inbreeding can have negative effects on animals. While a high degree of selectivity in breeding may give a particular advantage, in the long run it may not give the organism the wide range of adaptability needed to survive in a changing environment. Similar concerns raised about genetically engineered animals are well founded.

Then there is the problem of changing the pathogens to which a genetically engineered animal is host. If one engineers an animal to be resistant to a particular pathogen, the pathogen could mutate into a new form to which the animal is not resistant. Furthermore, such engineering can change the microenvironment of the pathogen, which "in turn could result in these pathogens becoming dangerous to humans or to other animals."[12]

Finally, there are three sets of safety problems. First, the altered animal could escape into an environment that was not anticipated and cause harm to other animals of the same species. Second, the humans doing the research could be harmed by exposure to dangerous material, either while doing the research or while studying the altered animal. Yet a third safety issue arises from the use of rBGH to increase milk production, an issue that itself has two impacts, one on the cows and the other on humans. Some veterinarians note that the use of this hormone puts stress on cows, which weakens their immune systems, leading to udder infections. This then leads to increased use of antibiotics to counter these infections.[13] The second impact affects consumers, who could be harmed by the increased levels of these antibiotic residues in the food chain.

Another consequence of the use of rBGH is an economic one. This hormone would increase an already existing surplus of milk, potentially driving the small dairy farmer out of business: "Better breeding, improved nutrition and a trend toward milking three times a day nearly tripled annual output per cow from 5,300 pounds in 1950 to 15,500 in 1993."[14]

These problems are thematically related to the issues raised in Chapter 2: safety, risk to animals and the environment, biodiversity, and the impact on humans. Again the resolution of many of these problems can come only from actually doing the research and carefully monitoring the results. Additionally, short-term testing can be done. For example, the FDA studied the use of bovine growth hormone in humans and concluded that "the data evaluated by the FDA documents the safety of food products from animals treated with rBGH. Bovine GH is biologically inactive in humans; therefore, residues of rBGH in food products would have no physiological effect even if absorbed intact from the gastrointestinal tract."[15] The FDA also concluded that there would be no impact on the nutritional quality of milk or on milk-based infant formulas. The FDA's position is that "the use of rBGH in dairy cattle presents no increased health risk to consumers."[16]

The Monsanto Corporation is now in the active phase of marketing this product under the name Posilac. Efforts to market the product have included a direct-mail campaign, a $150 voucher for a consultation with a veterinarian, and a $100 prize to farmers for each customer they refer.[17] Even though the FDA has approved the product, Monsanto's first-year sales were about $70 million, "a fraction of what Monsanto needs if Posilac is to pay off."[18] These sales figures will be important to watch since about 90 percent of Wisconsin's dairy farmers, for example, are either unlikely to use or will not use Posilac. Time will tell, first, if enough farmers think it is worth $5.80 per treated cow every other week to boost already increased milk production by another 5–15 percent and, second, if consumers will buy products made with milk from cows treated with Posilac.

The development and patenting of a bacterium by General Electric that disposes of oil slicks basically by eating them was the opening salvo in a debate over the development, use, ownership, and licensing of transgenic animals, a debate that was ultimately resolved in the Supreme Court decision *Diamond v. Chakrabarty*.[19] The editors of the *New York Times* weighed in by arguing that if one can own a cow, then why cannot one patent a cow too? They also argued that if it is acceptable to genetically engineer an animal, then patentability should be likewise acceptable.[20] The fact that the major premises of both arguments beg substantive questions seemed to be irrelevant to the editors, presumably in light of the current practice of owning animals and manipulating them genetically.

The move from patenting bacteria to patenting animals came with an application to patent a particular kind of Pacific oyster. Although the claim was rejected, the patent board for the case noted that the oyster did fall within the context of the Court's decision in the *Diamond* decision. Then the commissioner of patents and trademarks released a notice that the U.S. Patents and Trademark Office would consider "nonnaturally occurring nonhuman multicellular living organisms, including animals, to be patentable subject matter within the scope of 35 U.S.C. Para. 101."[21] Additionally, the notice stated that "the grant of a property right in a human was prohibited by the U.S. Constitution and that, therefore, any claim which included humans within its scope would not be considered patentable subject matter under 35 U.S.C. Para. 101."[22] In 1988, Harvard University received the first patent for a nonhuman mammal: a cancer-susceptible mouse. The debate consequently intensified.

The debate over patenting animals raised three particular issues. First is the sanctity of or reverence for life. Since the paradigm for patents is mechanical invention, will patenting lead us to think of animals as machines?[23] The key point is that "living things are distinguished by their having a certain kind of history rather than by their having a certain kind of composition."[24] But creating transgenic animals forces us to look at composition rather than origin. Should we separate the concept of being alive from that of being born, the concept of sanctity of life could be weakened, for we would return to the Cartesian position of seeing bodies as machines functioning autonomously.

The second issue is that the use of human DNA in animals highlights the point of "the moral category in which transgenic animals belong."[25] Robert Wachbroit raises the very interesting question of the use of such techniques on what he calls "higher animals" like monkeys or chimps: "How ought we to regard such a 'halfway' creature? As an augmented ape or as a diminished human?"[26] While the reality of such practices as the transfer of human embryos to animals for gestation and the creation of human-animal chimeras, or cross-species fertilization, is expressly prohibited by new National Institutes of Health (NIH) rules, the rules cover only research subsidized by the federal government and fears remain.[27]

The third issue emerging from the debate over patenting animals looks to a specific consequence: the cost of patented methods and materials. For example, Ohio University developed a patent for microinjection, "the process many scientists use to add new genes to mice."[28] DNX, a biotech company in Princeton, New Jersey, has the rights to the patent. Currently DNX does not ask for a fee to use the technique unless a commercial product is involved. But GenPharm International, a California-based biotech company, received a license from various universities to market knockout mice and charged customers between $80 and $100 per mouse. "The company also prohibited labs from breeding the mice, which effectively forced researchers to pay GenPharm for every mouse they used."[29] This type of pricing practice would obviously be prohibitive for many labs. The issue was resolved by GenPharm's decision to "allow researchers to breed as many mice as they want for an annual fee of $1,000 and the initial purchase of a breeding pair. One time breeding, to see if the pups have birth defects, for example, will be free."[30]

In March 1995, the European Parliament—with representatives from many Western European countries—closed a six-year debate by rejecting a directive that would have established common standards of patent protection for biotechnological inventions. Animal rights activists and environmentalists are pleased with this decision because they reject "the basic premise of the directive, that life is patentable."[31] Geneticists, however, are concerned because "the existing practice of patent offices may give commercial companies too much control over genetic data, thereby restricting research."[32] And some parliamentarians "opposed the directive because it would not have explicitly banned human germline gene therapy, which introduces permanent, inheritable traits into genes."[33] The patenting issues will now be resolved through precedents being built on a case-by-case basis. The fear is that this approach could "result in a patchwork of different regulations in different European countries."[34]

Almost all Americans are aware of the difficulties surrounding organ transplants. Problems such as the cost of the procedure and the rate of rejection, as well as the side effects of the drugs used to prevent rejection, are frequently discussed in the news. But the problem that receives the most attention is the shortage of organs for transplantation. In spite of media blitzes, public education campaigns, and legislation making donations easier, not nearly enough organs are donated to meet the increasing demand.

One of many responses to this problem has been the use of *xenografts*, tissue taken from animal species and grafted into human recipients. Thus for the attempts have focused on using animal organs—a baboon's heart or liver, for example—together with vast quantities of immunosuppressant drugs. The problem is that the human body can detect a stranger in its midst, so to speak, and begins a twofold defensive reaction. The first uses the immune system to reject the transplanted tissue; drugs such as cyclosporine are used to inhibit this reaction. The other defense is hyperacute rejection, a massive assault on the foreign tissue. "That reaction is now apparently the other great barrier to transplanting livers, hearts, kidneys and other organs from pigs to humans."[35]

Now a newer procedure is being reported. This strategy inserts the human immune system gene into pig embryos so that "the animals' organs [will] manufacture the chemicals that suppress human complement proteins."[36] The human immune system would then recognize the transplanted pig's organ as its own and would not mount the rejection defense. Two critical phases of the research have been completed: Transgenic mice "produce the suppressor molecules that nullify the effects of human complement when it is injected into them";[37] and transgenic pigs "grow up with organs that contain human complement chemicals and, in theory, a human immune system should be unable to distinguish these organs from human ones."[38] The next two steps would be to transplant organs to other primates, then to humans.

Although there is no suggestion at all that such a transgenic pig would be thought of as human or humanlike because of the presence of a particular gene, the technology does nonetheless reveal the potential for interspecies gene transfer, putting genes where no such genes have gone before. This type of research again forces the animal rights question because transgenic animals would be engineered, bred, and killed solely for the purpose of human well-being. The use of xenografts could also raise new questions about human identity and the integrity of the body.

Furthermore, questions about the safety of both animals and humans in transgenic engineering must be addressed, as must those about environmental impacts and the consequences of new genetic information on the animals themselves. And this technology sharply points to other traditional issues: animal rights, human dominance over other species, and the implications of patenting animals for both research and commercial development projects. Clearly the biotechnology community—as well as all its investors—has a lot to gain from such research, as might the public. And clearly animals will bear much of the burden for these gains. An example of this is the recent effort to demonstrate whether a particular gene called eyeless is indeed the gene responsible for the development of the eye. To test this, the gene was implanted on wings, legs, and antennae of the fruit fly. "The ectopic eyes appeared morphologically normal and consisted of groups of fully differentiated ommatidia with a complete set of photoreceptor cells."[39] Whether or not this effort caused physical harm to the fruit fly was unclear.

In sum, human well-being, economic development, and the welfare of animals and the environment are all in contention in the field of animal genetics. The resolution to these conflicts is far from clear.

NOTES

1. David Dickson, "No Patent for Harvard's Mouse?" *Science* 243 (24 February 1989): 1003.
2. Rudolf Jaenisch, "Transgenic Animals," *Science* 240 (10 June 1988): 1468–74. Though several years old, this article provides an excellent overview of the basic technologies and applications that are being developed presently.
3. Marcia Baringa, "Knockout Mice: Round Two," *Science* 265 (1 July 1994): 26.
4. Jean L. Marx, "Gene Watchers' Feast Served Up in Toronto," *Science* 242 (7 October 1988): 33.
5. Ibid.
6. Constance Holden, "Raising a Herd of Therapeutic Goats," *Science* 264 (13 May 1994): 902.
7. Ibid., 33.
8. *New York Times*, 11 March 1994, A19.
9. This phrase was coined by Dr. Solomon Katz, professor of biological anthropology at the University of Pennsylvania in Philadelphia, at a meeting on the "Theological and Ethical Implications of the Human Genome Initiative" sponsored by the Center for Theology and the Natural Sciences in Berkeley, California.
10. B. E. Rollin, "'The Frankenstein Thing': The Moral Impact of Genetic Engineering of Agricultural Animals on Society and Future Science," in *Genetic Engineering of Animals: An Agricultural Perspective*, ed. J. Warren Evans and Alexander Hollaender (New York: Plenum Press, 1988), 291.
11. Ibid.
12. Ibid., 292.
13. Kenneth Schneider, "U.S. Approves Use of Drug to Raise Milk Production," *New York Times*, 6 November 1993, A9.
14. Barnaby J. Feder, "Monsanto Has Its Wonder Hormone: Can It Sell It?" *New York Times*, 22 March 1995, F8.
15. Judith C. Juskevich and C. Greg Guyer, "Bovine Growth Hormone: Human Food Safety Evaluation," *Science* 249 (24 August 1990): 883.
16. Ibid.
17. Feder, "Monsanto," F8.
18. Ibid.
19. *Diamond v. Chakrabarty*, 206 USPQ 193 (1980). The issue presented to the Court was whether the "invention was a product of nature or an invention made by human intervention"; cited in Jeffery Auerbach, "Transgenic Animals and Patenting," *ATCC [American Type Culture Collection] Quarterly Newsletter* 9 (1989): 10.
20. "Yes, Patent Life," *New York Times*, 21 April 1987, A30.
21. Auerbach, "Transgenic Animals and Patenting," 10.
22. Ibid.
23. Robert Wachbroit, "Eight Worries About Patenting Animals," report sponsored by the Institute for Philosophy and Public Policy, 6.
24. Ibid.
25. Ibid., 8.
26. Ibid.
27. Eliot Marshall, "Rules on Embryo Research Due Out," *Science* 265 (19 August 1994): 1024.

28. David L. Wheeler, "Biologists Discuss Ways to 'Share' Genetically Engineered Mice," *Chronicle of Higher Education*, 7 April 1993, A14.
29. Christopher Anderson, "Researchers Win Decision on Knockout Mouse Pricing," *Science* 260 (2 April 1993): 23.
30. Ibid.
31. Claire O'Brien, "European Parliament Axes Patent Policy," *Science* 267 (10 March 1995): 1417.
32. Ibid.
33. Ibid., 1418.
34. Ibid., 1417.
35. Philip J. Hilts, "Gene Transfers Offer New Hope for Interspecies Organ Transplants," *New York Times*, 19 October 1993, C3.
36. Ibid.
37. Ibid.
38. Ibid.
39. Georg Hadler, Patrick Callaerts, and Walter J. Gehring, "Induction of Ectopic Eyes by Targeted Expression of the *eyeless* Gene in *Drosophila*," *Science* 267 (24 March 1995): 1788.

4

HUMANS AND THE NEW GENETICS

IN *THE REPUBLIC*, PLATO proposed a program of selective breeding to ensure the best quality of leaders. This program was limited in that it would be based on appearances and on social class and its success would take several years to determine. The fine-tuning such a program would require is provided in Aldous Huxley's *Brave New World*, where artificial reproductive and genetic engineering technologies have been perfected to mass-produce particular personalities for specific social functions.

In between the philosophical speculations of Plato and the dystopic musings of Huxley stand the "Fitter Family" competitions at state fairs sponsored by the America Eugenics Society.[1] These competitions, the first of which was held in 1920, were conducted in the human stock sections of state fairs and were intended to show how "the science of human husbandry must be developed based on the principles now followed by scientific agriculture, if the better elements of our civilization are to dominate or even survive."[2] Contestants had to provide a eugenic history, undergo a medical examination, and take an intelligence test. One of the exhibits at the Sesquicentennial Exposition in Philadelphia asked: "How long are we Americans going to be so careful for the pedigree of our pigs and chickens and cattle—and then leave the *ancestry of our children* to chance or to 'blind sentiment'?"[3]

This attitude, encouraged by both the British and American eugenics movements and given practical application by the Nationalist Socialist movement, was still dependent on traditional breeding methods and traditional Mendelian understandings of genetics. It was also undergirded by the joint assumptions of single-gene causality and the genetic heritability of all characteristics—physical or psychological.

The genetic dimension of speculations like these was to change dramatically with Watson and Crick's discovery of the structure of the DNA molecule in 1953. Twenty-some years after that, recombinant DNA technologies were discovered so that genetic information could be transferred from one organism to another without the constraints of reproduction or species boundaries. Another twenty years later, we have seen all the developments in plant

27

and animal husbandry discussed in the previous two chapters, as well as the first clinical trials of gene therapy. Although scientists recognize that much difficult work lies ahead, particularly because of increased awareness of multigene causality, the future of genetics nonetheless looks very bright and promising. Yet several issues are raised by all these developments, several of which we will now consider.

The Human Genome Project commenced in 1988. As previously mentioned, its purpose is to map and sequence the human genome, a task that is projected to take fifteen years at an estimated cost of $3 billion. The difficulty and enormity of the project is evidenced by the definition of *genome*:

> the totality of the DNA contained within the single chromosome of a bacterial species (or an individual bacterium) or within the diploid chromosome set of a eukaryotic species (or an individual eukaryote). The human genome, for example, consists of approximately 6 billion base pairs of DNA distributed among forty-six chromosomes. Sometimes the term "the human genome" is used to refer instead to the approximately 3 billion base pairs of DNA within the twenty-two different human autosomes and the human X and Y chromosomes.[4]

The genome is, in effect, all of the genetic information of an organism. Since the mission of the HGP is to map the 6 billion base pairs of DNA within the human chromosome structure, one can see that this is a fairly extensive project. The question is, what will be gained from it? Learning the sites of the base pairs—which is, after all, the primary purpose of the mapping project—will simply answer the location question, not the function question. Yet other information may be gleaned: the organization of genes, the way in which messages are coded and transmitted, and the function of so-called junk DNA, which appears to have no purpose.

These are technical issues that will take time to examine and answer. But there is one question that occasionally emerges in discussions of the genome project that has to do with the status of the human genome: Will the human genome take on a normative status? That is, will the map of the genome function socially, medically, or politically as the normative profile of the human? Will it serve as a type of genetic Procrustean bed against which individuals will be measured? This issue has particular importance in genetic medicine and in prenatal diagnosis, where decisions are based on the genetic profile of the fetus and on the medical and social consequences (or assumed consequences) of the genetic profile of the fetus.

The HGP was "sold" to the U.S. Congress and to the American people on the promise of many benefits, the most typical of which was curing disease through genetic interventions. While it is true that genes that cause particular diseases have been discovered—for instance, the gene for Huntington's disease—the transition from discovery to treatment, let alone to cure, is still many years away. The problem is the gap between promise and delivery. Although this gap is frustrating to scientists and clinicians, it is even more so to individuals with diseases. And it may be equally frustrating to Congress, which is asked annually to increase the HGP budget but does not see a practical payoff. The issue is not whether the HGP will produce a payoff in terms of relieving human misery; it will. Rather, the issue is that the gap between discovery and therapy tends to obscure long-term benefits.

The HGP will undoubtedly produce a map of the human genome, a major application of which will be in both genetic screening programs and prenatal diagnosis. Once the location of a gene that causes a particular problem is known, the next step is discovering who carries that gene. In the past, massive screening programs have attempted to identify carriers of Tay-Sachs disease, sickle-cell anemia, phenylketonuria (PKU), and other genetic diseases. Since Tay-Sachs and sickle-cell anemia are generally linked with the Jewish and African American communities, respectively, concerns about racism and genocide were raised. Moreover, fears were raised about possible discrimination against individuals identified as having the gene for such diseases. Confusion about the difference between being a carrier and having the disease also caused public confusion. For example, even though carriers of sickle-cell anemia do not suffer the symptoms of the disease, African American members of the U.S. Air Force were, for a time, prohibited from being pilots for fear of the consequences of an oxygen shortage during a flight. Furthermore, the topics of confidentiality and informed consent invariably cropped up throughout the screening efforts. The combined weight of all these concerns, together with cost factors and low frequency rates, eventually led to the elimination of the programs.

Now, a new variation of prenatal and even preimplantation genetic screening is available because of developments in genetics coupled with those of in vitro fertilization (IVF). One or two cells are removed from a preimplantation embryo at either the eight- or the sixteen-cell stage of development. These cells are then analyzed to determine if the particular disease in question is present. Only those preimplantation embryos without the disease are then transferred to the uterus.

Since this preimplantation technology is expensive and is associated with the difficulties inherent to achieving pregnancy through IVF, postimplantation diagnostic technologies will remain a common method of prenatal screening. But the most common method is amniocentesis, in which amniotic fluid is withdrawn from the uterus toward the end of the first trimester. Fetal cells are removed from the fluid, cultured, and analyzed for particular diseases. Other technologies being used are chorionic villus sampling (CVS), the alpha-fetoprotein test (AFT), and fluorescent in situ hybridization (FISH).

CVS examines cells taken from the chorion, the fingerlike projections surrounding the membrane around the fetus. The advantage of this test is that it can be performed much earlier in the pregnancy than amniocentesis, and, consequently, diagnostic information can be obtained earlier. AFP involves obtaining a blood sample from the pregnant woman to determine if there are abnormal levels of the alpha-fetoprotein. High levels indicate the possibility of neurological damage to the fetus. In this case, further testing is required, though normal levels eliminate the need for additional testing. FISH involves a set of "DNA probes that home in on regions of five chromosomes—21, 18, 13, X, and Y—which together account for 90% of all birth defects related to chromosomal abnormalities."[5] The probes are equipped with a fluorescent dye, each of which glows with a different color depending on exposure to specific ultraviolet lights. Extra copies of a chromosome can therefore be easily detected. The test will not replace traditional amniocentesis, but it can be used for preliminary screening and cuts the waiting time from three weeks to less than two days.[6]

Past screening efforts have focused on diagnosis and attempted cures once a disease manifested itself in an individual. Steps are now being taken to develop therapies that will attack a disease at the most basic level and cause—the gene—thus preventing the disease from manifesting itself at all. "On 19 January [1989] the United States crossed the threshold into the much debated but still uncharted world of human gene therapy."[7] After seven months of exhaustive review, the federal government approved introduction of a foreign gene into humans. This protocol involved inserting a marker gene into ten terminally ill patients to trace the progress of an experimental cancer therapy.

Though not technically gene therapy, the protocol is a precursor to it, and its approval caused the expected debate. Not only are the traditional ethical research questions of risk-benefit analysis, informed consent, and the like, at issue here; there is also the question of social implications, which are much more difficult to phrase correctly, much less evaluate. Nonetheless, the eugenics movement hovers in the background, accompanied by its possible applications. Rifkin evoked the image of a slippery slope leading to outcomes that could not be controlled. He also raised "the specter of 'engineering' workers to render them less susceptible to chemical carcinogens in lieu of cleaning up the workplace,"[8] a strategy reminiscent of Huxley's reproductive program.

In September 1990, the first federally sponsored gene therapy experiment occurred. In this experiment, "a team of doctors introduced into [the female research subject's] blood stream some 1 billion cells, each containing a copy of a foreign gene. If all goes well, these genes will begin producing ADA [adenosine deaminase], the essential enzyme she requires, and her devastated immune system will slowly begin to recover."[9] Four years later the therapy was working and the subject was developing a normal immune system. This pioneering work was done by Drs. Kenneth Culver, R. Michael Blaese, and W. French Anderson, who in particular has become the most eloquent—and most persistent—spokesperson for gene therapy.[10]

Even more controversial than germ-line modifications is the fierce debate over genes and behavior. This debate is not a simplistic rehashing of the traditional nature/nurture dichotomy. Nor does it resurrect the racist ideology that fueled the 1924 United States Immigration Restriction Act, which was designed to prevent the deterioration of the Nordic (i.e., "real" American) stock. Nor is it an attempt to regenerate the eugenicists' fantasies and programs of the 1930s. Rather, the real debate is over the efforts of many to examine as scientifically and as morally responsibly as possible the actual relation, if any, between genes and behavior. What distinguishes this debate from previous ones is the abandonment of both a simplistic understanding of the Mendelian genetics model and the assumption that all characteristics—physical and psychological—are inherited through the genes. In place of this is a multigenetic model as well as the recognition of the many and complex interactions between genes and the environment.

Yet, despite the care with which the new research is being carried on, flash points emerge and controversies erupt. In May 1992, for example, the NIH awarded a grant for a conference entitled "Genetic Factors in Crime: Findings, Uses, and Implications." In July the funds for the conference were suspended "after a number of critics, in particular a group that included Howard University political scientist Ronald Walters, complained that the topic of the conference was racist in its implications."[11] The conference organizer, David Wasserman of the University of Maryland, made various changes and resubmitted the proposal. In September, the proposal was again rejected.

In July 1993, a research article was published in *Science* entitled "A Linkage Between DNA Markers on the X Chromosome and Male Sexual Orientation."[12] It was accompanied by a review essay titled "Evidence for Homosexuality Gene." A flurry of articles discussing various aspects of the "gay gene" soon appeared, mainly denouncing the research. Ruth Hubbard, professor emeritus of biology at Harvard University, said, "This study, like similar previous findings, is flawed. It is based on simplistic assumptions about sexuality and is hampered by the near impossibility of establishing links between genes and behavior."[13] In an instance of art imitating life, the play *Twilight of the Golds* opened on Broadway in October 1993. This play "is about a couple who discover through a prenatal test that their baby boy is destined to be a homosexual and then wrestle with themselves and their families over whether to abort the fetus."[14] In addition to the question of the appropriate use of prenatal diagnosis, the other buried question in this particular case may be an unstated assumption that a genetic marker for homosexuality may also be a marker for a "homosexual lifestyle," whatever that might be.

Thus the stage is set for a new and intense debate over the issue of behavior and genetics. However, the context has changed somewhat and needs careful examination.

The application of modern genetics to humans is exciting and complex, both scientifically and ethically. While many of the traditional ethical values of privacy, autonomy, and freedom remain a context in which much of the new genetics will be discussed, developing and more subtle issues will force the nuances of these values and their applications to the level of more contentious problems. Developments in plant and animal gene applications will suggest human applications. Individual and social desires for improved health and enhanced capacities will drive pressure for applications. Claims and promises will continue to outstrip the reality of genetic medicine, as they always have.

Yet we stand on the brink of major breakthroughs in genetics. The continuing issue is whether we will have the wisdom to evaluate, monitor, and apply these discoveries not only for the good of particular individuals, but for the well-being of all of society.

NOTES

1. Daniel J. Kevles, *In the Name of Eugenics: Genetics and the Uses of Human Heredity* (New York: Alfred A. Knopf, 1985), 61.
2. Ibid., 62.
3. Ibid., 62–3.
4. "The Human Genome Project," *Los Alamos Science* 20 (1992): 333. In this definition, the term *eukarote* refers to species in which cell division occurs in specific ways: One-celled organisms reproduce asexually, or multicellular organisms increase and replace dead cells. The cell division occurs through mitosis in which the daughter cells are genetically identical to the mother cell. *Autosomes* is another term for all chromosomes in eukarotic species other than the sex chromosomes.
5. Leslie Roberts, "FISHing Cuts the Angst in Amniocentesis," *Science* 254 (1991): 378.
6. Ibid.
7. Leslie Roberts, "Ethical Questions Haunt New Genetic Technologies," *Science* 243 (1989): 1134.
8. Ibid., 1135.
9. Leon Jaroff, "Giant Step for Gene Therapy," *Time*, 24 September 1990, 74.
10. W. French Anderson, "Human Gene Therapy," *Science* 256 (1992): 808.
11. Constance Holden, "Back to the Drawing Board, Says NIH," *Science* 257 (1992).
12. Dean H. Hammer et al., "A Linkage Between DNA Markers on the X Chromosome and Male Sexual Orientation," *Science* 262 (1993): 321–7.
13. Ruth Hubbard, "False Genetic Markers," *New York Times*, 2 August 1993, A15.
14. Natalie Angier, "Playing God, with Science as a Midwife," *New York Times*, 17 October 1993, H9.

ROMAN CATHOLIC PERSPECTIVES ON GENETIC ENGINEERING

THE ROMAN CATHOLIC CHURCH uses a set of official teachings on genetics coming from various levels of the hierarchy—the official magisterium or teaching authority of the church, which includes the pope, bishops, and several councils. It also uses reflections on those teachings by various Vatican congregations and theologians. This chapter will present a sampling of these perspectives under the headings of various themes: theological anthropology, limitations on genetic interventions, and justifications for genetic interventions.[1] This format serves two purposes: First, we will see how common themes are discussed from a variety of perspectives; second, we will be able to sample representative ideas on genetic engineering in a coherent fashion.

THEOLOGICAL ANTHROPOLOGY

Theological anthropology considers the nature of human beings in relation to their divine origins. Examining this theme from the Roman Catholic perspective will provide us with Catholicism's vision of the human, as well as a basis for the development of further perspectives on ethics.

In the modern period, Pope Pius XII was one of the first popes to speak directly to issues of genetics—hence the importance of his anthropological perspectives. Pius XII discussed several themes related to genetics, the first of which has to do with nature and the law of nature. Pius affirmed an order created by God that is "directed to the end designed by the Creator. It embrace[s] not only the external acts of man, but also the internal consent of his free will."[2] This order sets limits on what the individual can do: "Man, in truth, is not the owner of his body nor its absolute lord, but only its user";[3] thus this natural order governs what can and cannot be done to or with the body.

In another context, Pius XII expressed this "stewardship ethic" accordingly:

As far as the patient is concerned, he is not absolute master of himself, of his body, or of his soul. He cannot, therefore, freely dispose of himself as

he pleases. Even the motive for which he acts is not by itself either sufficient or determining. The patient is bound by the immanent purposes fixed
by nature. He possesses the right to use, limited by natural finality, the
faculties and powers of his human nature.[4]

This view of the human defines a narrow range of opportunities for intervention, but it does not totally eliminate them.

Vatican Council II also presented its vision of the human in relation to
God, as well as giving a context within which to evaluate our broader concerns. The council noted that human mastery has extended over almost the
whole of nature. In itself this type of activity is part of God's will: "For
man, created to God's image, received a mandate to subject to himself the
earth and all that it contains, and to govern the world with justice and holi-
ness."[5] The council drew this conclusion: "Hence it is clear that men are not
deterred by the Christian message from building up the world, or impelled
to neglect the welfare of their fellows. They are, rather, more stringently
bound to do these very things."[6] This view of human nature also recognizes
limits on human activity, yet it argues that there is an obligation to engage in
worldly activities to help "build up," or improve, the world in which we live.

The current pope, John Paul II, has made theological anthropology a strong
feature of his teachings. For example, in his book *Love and Responsibility*,
written while he was still Cardinal Karol Wojtyla, we find the framework
for his later thought. The heart of the moral order has its origin in justice to
God and is based on the fact of creation. The order of nature has its origin
in God "since it rests directly on the essences (or natures) of existing creatures, from which arise all dependencies, relationships and connections between them."[7] Thus the order of nature grounds morality.

> In the world of human beings the dictates of the natural order are realized
> in a different way—they must be understood and rationally accepted. *And
> this understanding and rational acceptance of the order of nature—is at
> the same time recognition of the rights of the Creator.* Elementary justice
> on the part of man towards God is founded on it. Man is just towards
> God the Creator when he recognizes the order of nature and conforms to
> it in his actions.[8]

Or, as John Paul puts it in another way: "But before and above all else
man's conscience, his immediate guide in all his doings, must be in harmony with the law of nature. When it is, man is just towards the Creator."[9]
This view makes the human an active participant in the order of nature, for
in a classic statement on the issue, "Man, by understanding the order of
nature and conforming to it in his actions, participates in the thought of
God, becomes *particeps Creatoris*, has a share in the law which God be-
stowed on the world when he created it at the beginning of time."[10]

The pope distinguishes between the order of nature and the biological order. The order of nature is the "divine order inasmuch as it is realized under the continuous influence of God the Creator."[11] The biological order, however, is the "same as the order of nature but only in so far as this is accessible to the methods of empirical and descriptive natural science":[12] It is not a specific order of existence with its own relation to God but a physical description of the natural order created and structured by God. Within the natural order, the human has a structure. Humans are "only required not to destroy or squander . . . natural resources, but to use them with restraint, so as not to impede the development of man himself, and so as to ensure the coexistence of human societies in justice and harmony."[13] While not rejecting the vision of Vatican Council II, this view of the human vocation within the world is more attuned with the vision of Pius XII, who also focused on the nature of objective structure of creation, which both situates the human within a moral universe and establishes the basis for moral behavior.

The theme of theological anthropology has also been developed by several theologians. Among the first to pursue this systematically was Karl Rahner, S.J., one of the major contributors to the theology of Vatican II and one of the most significant theologians of the twentieth century. First, let us examine his perspectives on human nature.

Christian anthropology defines the human as a self-creating being, a "free being before God, a person subject to himself and capable of freely determining his own final condition. This self-determination is so complete that he can ultimately and absolutely become what he wants to be."[14] Thus as created, the human is essentially unfinished and attains self-determination through free action. What Rahner contributes to the discourse is how the power of self-creation "has now grasped the physical, psychological, and sociological dimensions of [man's] existence."[15] We have now therefore become free beings under our "own responsible control."[16] And this self-creation will "develop the concrete form of human openness which leads to the absolute future that comes from God."[17] However, this self-creation can have irreversible consequences. Christian anthropology puts us on guard against the dangers involved: "The fall initiated a process that allowed for no return."[18]

Such a self-creation proceeds from respect for nature and yet helps form human nature. Critical for Rahner is that the nature that must be respected "is a nature still being actively formed by man himself through self-creation."[19] Human nature, then, is not something fixed or given. Our understanding of human nature will be experienced in no "other way than in a particular historical form, where we are unable to distinguish clearly and unequivocally between the nature 'in itself' and its concrete variable form [?]."[20]

An important counterpoint to the theme of self-creation is Rahner's insistence that there is another radical *existentiale*, or structure of existence, that sets a limit to planning: The human "is no less a being whose essence has been predetermined";[21] that is, the human has not called him or herself into existence. We have not chosen our world but, rather, have "been projected into a particular world and . . . this world is presented to [us] for [our] free acceptance."[22] The very important conclusion—and the basis of the limit of self-creation—is that "the world can never be 'worked over' to such an extent that man is eventually dealing only with material *he* has chosen and created."[23] For Rahner, then, a given factor of human nature is that "accepting this necessarily alien determination of one's own being *is* and *remains*, therefore, a fundamental task of man in his free moral existence."[24] In concrete terms this means that "genetic manipulation is the embodiment of the fear of oneself, the fear of accepting one's self as the unknown quantity it is."[25] And the driving force behind genetic manipulation, from this perspective of the limit on our nature, is "despair because he cannot *dispose* of existence."[26]

There is tension in the Rahnerian perspective. While the human is called to self-creation in radical freedom through which the absolute future who is God is encountered, there is a clear limit to self-creation: the radical givenness of the human condition that prohibits a radical disposal of ourselves. This leads to the rather somber conclusion that "if the new humanity of the future is to survive, it must cultivate a sober and critical resistance to the fascination of novel possibilities."[27]

Bernard Häring, C.S.S.R., a German moral theologian, is one of the major contributors to the reform of moral theology in Catholicism, as well as a major contributor to Vatican II. A clear position on human nature informs Häring's vision:

> The fundamental condition for being truly free while acting as manipulator of the world around is our sabbath, our repose before God. Only if man transcends himself and recognizes the gratuity of all creation and of his own call to be a co-creator, can he submit the earth to his own dignity.[28]

This foundation gives us the ability to keep a sense of admiration and adoration, without which, Häring says, "our manipulation of the world becomes depletion and alienation."[29] Our vocation is to become a co-creator and co-revealer through uniting with the human community to enhance the "freedom and co-responsibility of all mankind."[30] In so transforming the world, the person does not act merely as a consumer or manipulator; rather, the person is "an artist, and he grows in awareness and dignity while transforming the work, provided he sees his highest creativity in mutual respect and reverence in all his human relations."[31]

In Häring's vision, freedom plays a large role. Inner personal freedom is the "capacity to long for ever-growing knowledge of what is good and truthful, the capacity to love what is good and put it into practice."[32] Critical elements of this are our own "self-interpretation, self-awareness, and active insertion into the history of liberation."[33] This becomes a critical touchstone in assessing the ethics of a particular manipulation.

Richard McCormick, S.J., a leading American moral theologian who teaches at the University of Notre Dame, has provided a general overview of critical ethical themes that serves as a context in which to present his own analysis. He has six themes that ought to inform our bioethical reasoning. First is the recognition that life is a basic, but not an absolute, good.[34] Life itself can cede to other values: the glory of God, the salvation of souls, or service to one's neighbor. Second, a vision of the value of life must inform Christian reflections about nascent life and, therefore, a "simple pro-choice *moral* position is in conflict with the biblical story."[35] Third, in the Christian perspective, "the meaning, substance, and consummation of life are found in *human relationships*."[36] Life is to be valued as a condition for other values, and since these values cluster around human relations, life is a value to be preserved "only insofar as it contains some potentiality for human relationships."[37] Fourth, our well-being is pursued only interdependently. Sociality is an essential part of both our being and our becoming. Fifth, the spheres of life giving and love making are not to be radically put asunder. McCormick's emphasis here is on the spheres of the relationship as a whole, not on the isolated acts of a couple. Sixth, "heterosexual, permanent marriage" is seen as "normative."[38] By this McCormick means that "monogamous marriage provides us with our best chance to humanize our sexuality and bridge the separateness and isolation of our individual selves."[39]

These principles provide the foundation upon which to present the specific analysis of McCormick's discussion of genetic engineering later in this chapter. While they do not exhaust McCormick's thinking on these topics, they are nevertheless touchstones to which he continually refers for his analysis.

Charles Curran, another major Catholic American moral theologian who is currently teaching at Southern Methodist University, has written frequently and widely. Curran's moral method "consists of a perspective based on the fivefold Christian mysteries of creation, sin, incarnation, redemption, and resurrection destiny."[40] This stance provides a positive methodology and perspective.

> Creation indicates the goodness of the human and human reason; but sin touches all reality, without, however, destroying the basic goodness of creation. Incarnation integrates all reality into the plan of God's kingdom. Redemption as already present affects all reality, while resurrection destiny as future exists in continuity with the redeemed present but also in discontinuity because the fullness of the kingdom remains God's gracious gift at the end of time.[41]

Curran's model of the Christian life is relationality-responsibility, which views "the moral life primarily in terms of the person's multiple relationships with God, neighbor, world, and self and the subject's actions in this context."[42] This reflects the Christian emphasis on covenant and love. It emphasizes the need to respond to the contemporary situation and make the Kingdom of God more present. And this approach also opens up different approaches to particular questions. Curran develops a Christian anthropology that emphasizes the person in a twofold way: "First, individual actions come from the person and are expressive of the person. . . . Second, the person, through one's actions, develops and constitutes oneself as a moral subject."[43] Additionally, our basic relationship to ourself is governed by "the basic attitude of stewardship, using our gifts, talents, and selves in the living out of the Christian life."[44]

Finally, Curran uses a theory of compromise to help resolve ethical conflicts. This refers to "cases in which the presence of sin might justify an action which could not be justified if sin and its effects were not present."[45] Compromise tries to "describe the reality in order to recognize the tension between justifying such actions because of the presence of sin and the Christian obligation to overcome sin and its effects."[46]

In their book *Health Care Ethics*, Benedict Ashley, O.P., and Kevin O'Rourke, O.P., both moral theologians at St. Louis University, present a comprehensive overview of several issues in genetic engineering. They note that the classic way of beginning discussions of genetic engineering is with human dominion over nature. While recognizing the role this dimension has had, Ashley and O'Rourke present two problems with it. First, it is "too much influenced by the Greek image of God as a jealous monarch who became angry when Prometheus infringed on his prerogatives."[47] Alternatively, others see attempts to improve the human "as an insult to the work of the Creator whose masterpiece is man, or at least as a fatal temptation to pride."[48]

The perspective Ashley and O'Rourke propose focuses on three dimensions. First is the fact that God is a generous creator who, in creating humans, "called them by the gift of intelligence to share in his creative power."[49] Second is the affirmation of a universe created through an evolutionary process that is not yet complete. Thus God has made us "co-workers and encourages [us] to exercise real originality."[50] Third is the fact that our creativity is dependent on our brain. Therefore "any alteration that would injure the brain and hence a person's very creativity would indeed be disastrous mutilation, especially if this were to be transmitted genetically."[51]

James Keenan, S.J., who teaches moral theology at Weston Jesuit School of Theology in Cambridge, Massachusetts, discusses the question of what is morally new in genetic engineering by identifying what is for him a critical shift: from a rights-based model to a virtue model. Within this broader framework of the methodology of moral theology, Keenan discusses several features of his theological anthropology.

He argues that the newness of genetic engineering is that we are redirecting the evolution of our world and of humans, not from without but from within. Consequently, "just as the process of directing nature has caused us to objectify nature, so too the development of eugenics requires us to objectify the human subject."[52] This is the primary moral issue because we either objectify a person for treatment or, in redesigning the genotype either for therapy or for enhancement, we objectify the potential human subject. Such possibilities also affect the parent-child bond because of the presumed rights to have a child and even to have a child with certain characteristics. Such tendencies contribute to the objectification of the child and to the depersonalization of parenthood.

Keenan further develops the issue of objectification by arguing that in genetics, "the discoveries of the human body as relational and as intergenerational further our understanding of the body not as matter or object, but as disposed to being subject."[53] The "link between person and genotype is found in the human body," and "the notion of person is inclusive of the human body."[54] Keenan's concern is to argue that a critical danger in genetics is "the failure to see the human body as subject and . . . the potential for treating the human body as the object of our wishes."[55] An important conclusion follows from this perspective: "The human genome itself is dispositive to being a subject (and not an object) to the extent that it is dispositively a human body."[56] For Keenan, this is not simply a descriptive statement but a moral claim. The substantive moral claim is that "the living human body deserves to be treated as a subject."[57]

LIMITATIONS ON GENETIC INTERVENTIONS

A second major theme in Roman Catholic perspectives on genetic interventions and engineering is the limits on such interventions. These limits are drawn from the theological anthropology just discussed. For example, Pius XII noted that

> where man is concerned, genetics is always dealing with personal beings, with inviolable rights, with individuals who, for their part, are bound by unshakeable moral laws, in using their power to raise up a new life. Thus the Creator Himself has established certain barriers in the moral domain, which no human power has authority to remove.[58]

On this basis, Pius condemned the eugenics movement, all forms of artificial insemination, in vitro fertilization, direct sterilization, and the prohibition of marriage to those with genetic illness. In short, Pius, on the basis of natural law, prohibited any interference with the physical act of heterosexual married intercourse. The basis for the morality of heterosexual married intercourse—as well as for any study or use of genetic material—is the biological integrity of the physical act of intercourse. Any attempt at interference is considered stepping outside the bounds imposed by nature and constitutes a violation of the stewardship ethic.

Vatican Council II also spoke to the issue of human limitations when it provided some ethical guidelines for the building up of the world. For example, the council proposed as the norm of human activity "that in accord with the divine plan and will, it should harmonize with the genuine good of the human race, and allow men as individuals and as members of society to pursue their total vocation and fulfill it."[59] This was further specified by the assertion that by the very fact of being created, "all things are endowed with their own stability, truth, goodness, proper laws, and order. Man must respect these as he isolates them by the appropriate methods of the individual science or arts."[60]

The council is walking a fine line here. On the one hand, the council's document, *Gaudium et Spes*, asserts strongly the legitimate autonomy of created reality: "We cannot but deplore certain habits of mind, sometimes found too among Christians, which do not sufficiently attend to the rightful independence of science."[61] But such autonomy does not mean that created things do not depend on God or that "man can use them without any reference to the Creator."[62] Thus there is an affirmation of natural law, but it is conditioned somewhat by the emphasis on the integrity of created reality.

The tension in this position is shown clearly when the document discusses human reproduction:

> Therefore when there is a question of harmonizing conjugal love with the responsible transmission of life, the moral aspect of any procedure does not depend solely on sincere intentions or on an evaluation of motives. It must be determined by objective standards.[63]

As such this statement is close to the teaching of Pius XII. But the text goes on to say that these standards must be "based on the nature of the human person and his acts."[64] This part of the criterion, while rooted in the tradition, opens the way to a consideration of the person that incorporates more than the biology of his or her acts.

While no specific statement on genetics was made in *Gaudium et Spes*, one quotation does provide an orientation with which to consider it:

> For God, the Lord of life, has conferred on men, the surpassing ministry of safeguarding life—a ministry which must be fulfilled in a manner which is worthy of man. Therefore from the moment of its conception life must be guarded with the greatest care, while abortion and infanticide are unspeakable crimes. The sexual characteristics of man and the final faculty

of reproduction wonderfully exceed the dispositions of lower forms of life. . . . Relying on these principles, sons of the Church may not undertake methods of regulating procreation which are found blameworthy by the teaching authority of the Church in its unfolding of the divine law.[65]

Pope Paul VI also spoke to the issue of limits. Though his comments were made primarily within the area of human reproduction, they set a framework that has implications for genetic interventions insofar as they show the basis on which interventions must be justified. Paul VI specified the content of the law of nature and the ethics of stewardship in the encyclical *Humanae Vitae*. Although its focus is the ethics of heterosexual married reproduction, the argument on which the encyclical is based is critical in understanding many of the themes of his perspective. Central to the argument is the notion of responsible parenthood. This concept is related to three circumstances. First is the biological dimension, which "means the knowledge and respect of [sexual organ] functions; human intellect discovers in the poser of giving life biological laws which are part of the human person."[66] Second is the instinctual dimension, which means "that necessary dominion which reason and will must exercise over [instinct and passion]."[67] Finally there is the socioeconomic dimension, which either accepts the children born to the family or which, for a time and in accord with the moral law, avoids a new birth.

Critical to the argument is the "inseparable connection, willed by God and unable to be broken by man on his own initiative, between the two meanings of the conjugal act: the unitive meaning and the procreative meaning."[68] Such a structure "capacitates them for the generation of new lives, according to laws inscribed in the very being of man and of woman."[69] Of importance in developing the ethic surrounding human reproduction is the following comment:

> To make use of the gift of conjugal love while respecting the laws of the generative process means to acknowledge oneself not to be the arbiter of the sources of human life, but rather the minister of the design established by the Creator. In fact, just as man does not have unlimited dominion over his body in general, so also, with particular reason, he has no such dominion over his generative faculties as such, because of their instinctive ordination toward raising up life, of which God is the principle.[70]

This affirmation of an inherent limit to human action based on the physical structure of the person is further specified later in the encyclical:

> Consequently, if the mission of generating life is not to be exposed to the arbitrary will of men, one must necessarily recognize unsurmountable limits to the possibility of man's domination over his own body and its functions; limits which no man, whether a private individual or one invested with authority, may licitly surpass. And such limits cannot be determined

otherwise than by the respect due to the integrity of the human organism and its functions, according to the principles recalled earlier, and also according to the correct understanding of the "principle of totality" illustrated by our predecessor Pope Pius XII.[71]

Thus Paul VI clearly invoked a particular understanding of the nature of the human person and a standard of morality based on that nature as a way of identifying the limits to human activity and dominion. Biological structures morally qualify human activity since disregarding them violates the order willed by God in the creation of human beings.

Pope John Paul II also specified the limits of human intervention. The immediate context of these statements is human reproduction, but the pope also uses this framework to address issues in genetic engineering. As explained earlier, the pope distinguishes between the biological order and the order of nature, and within the natural order, humans have a structure that, on the one hand, requires them to not impede the development of their race. On the other hand, however, man's "sexual urge is connected in a special way with the natural order of existence, which is the divine order."[72] And that determines the proper purpose of the sexual urge. Thus "it is not the love of man and woman that determines the proper purpose of the sexual urge. The proper end of the urge, the end *per se*, is something suprapersonal, the existence of the species Homo, the constant prolongation of its existence."[73] Such a respect for the order of nature sets out the following perspective:

> Marriage, objectively considered, must provide first of all the means of continuing existence, secondly a conjugal life for man and woman, and thirdly a legitimate orientation for desire. The ends of marriage, in the order mentioned, are incompatible with any subjectivist interpretation of the sexual urge, and therefore demand from man, as a person, objectivity in his thinking on sexual matters, and above all in his behavior. This objectivity is the foundation of conjugal morality.[74]

Thus morality in general and in marriage in particular consists of active conformity to the order of nature through which humans participate in the plan of God for creation and become participants in the very act of creation. Two conclusions follow from this. First, with respect to marriage,

> When couples, by means of recourse to contraception, separate these two meanings [the unitive and the procreative] that God the Creator has inscribed in the being of man and woman in the dynamism of their sexual communion, they act as "arbiters" of the divine plan and they "manipulate" and degrade human sexuality—and with it themselves and their married partner—by altering its value of "total" self-giving.[75]

Second, with respect to public policy,

> Thus the Church condemns as a grave offense against human dignity and justice all those activities of human governments or other public authorities which attempt to limit in any way the freedom of couples in deciding about children. Consequently, any violence applied by such authorities in favor of contraception or, still worse, of sterilization and procured abortion, must be altogether condemned and forcefully rejected.[76]

Finally, Pope John Paul II condemns "in the most explicit and formal way experimental manipulations of the human embryo, since the human being, from conception to death, cannot be exploited for any purpose whatsoever."[77] Thus the criterion of the exploitation of the human imposes a clear limit on experimentation.

The Congregation for the Doctrine of the Faith, a Vatican congregation charged with maintaining the correctness of the Catholic faith, issued a major statement regarding human reproduction, *Donum Vitae*, in 1987. This document also relies on the natural law tradition as the foundation of its moral analysis. The natural moral law is defined as "the rational order whereby man is called by the Creator to direct and regulate his life and action and in particular to make use of his own body."[78] Two norms particularly identified for ethical analysis are the life of the human being and the special nature of the transmission of life in marriage.

The statements about human life have several dimensions. First is the affirmation that "from the moment of conception, the life of every human being is to be respected in an absolute way because man is the only creature on earth that God has 'wished for himself' and the spiritual soul of each man is 'immediately created' by God."[79] Second, since God is the Lord of life from beginning to end, "No one can in any circumstance claim for himself the right to destroy directly an innocent human being."[80] Finally, an intervention "on the human body affects not only the tissues, the organs and their functions, but also involves the person himself on different levels. It involves, therefore, perhaps in an implicit but nonetheless real way, a moral significance and responsibility."[81]

With respect to the transmission of human life, *Donum Vitae* affirms

> the "inseparable connection, willed by God and unable to be broken by man on his own initiative, between the two meanings of the conjugal act: the unitive meaning and the procreative meaning. Indeed, by its intimate structure the conjugal act, while most closely uniting husband and wife capacitates them for the generation of new lives according to laws inscribed in the very being of man and of woman." This principle, which is based upon the nature of marriage and the intimate connection of the goods of marriage, has well-known consequences on the level of responsible

fatherhood and motherhood. "By safeguarding both these essential aspects, the unitive and the procreative, the conjugal act preserves in its fullness the sense of true mutual love and its ordination toward man's exalted vocation to parenthood."[82]

Because of the moral significance of the links between the conjugal act and the goods of marriage, the unity of the person and the dignity of his or her origin, "the procreation of a human person [must] be brought about as the fruit of the conjugal act specific to the love between spouses."[83] Therefore, "No one may subject the coming of a child into the world to conditions of technical efficiency which are to be evaluated according to standards of control and dominion."[84]

While the implications of this for all sorts of artificial reproduction are obvious, these two principles also speak to the issue of genetic testing and fetal research. Prenatal diagnosis is morally licit if it "respects the life and integrity of the embryo and the human fetus and is directed toward its safe-guarding or healing as an individual."[85] Thus any link of prenatal diagnosis to direct abortion is prohibited, and prenatal diagnosis is morally permissible "with the consent of the parents after they have been adequately in-formed, if the methods employed safeguard the life and integrity of the embryo and the mother, without subjecting them to disproportionate risks."[86]

Therapeutic procedures on the embryo are morally permissible if they "respect the life and integrity of the embryo and do not involve disproportionate risks for it, but are directed toward its healing, the improvement of its condition of health or its individual survival."[87] Research or experimentation can be performed on embryos and fetuses if "there is a moral certainty of not causing harm to the life or integrity of the unborn child and the mother, and on condition that the parents have given their free and informed consent to the procedure."[88] Additionally, living embryos, viable or not, "must be respected just like any other human person; experimentation on embryos which is not directly therapeutic is illicit."[89]

Finally, embryos may not be produced in vitro to be used for experimentation, nor may embryos obtained in this way for research be destroyed because "by acting in this way the researcher usurps the place of God; and, even though he may be unaware of this, he sets himself up as the master of the destiny of others inasmuch as he arbitrarily chooses whom he will allow to live and whom he will send to death and kills defenseless human beings."[90]

Rahner also developed a perspective on limitations on human action, primarily in the context of artificial insemination and in vitro fertilization. His comments are a critique of both. Rahner argues against these interventions because this manipulation "fundamentally separates the marital union from the procreation of a new person as this permanent embodiment of the unity of married love; and it transfers procreation, isolated and torn from its human matrix, to an area outside man's sphere of intimacy."[91] Additionally, such a manipulation reflects a desire to plan the human totally and, as such, represents a transgression of the *existentiale* that rejects our total disposability. Finally, Rahner sees a most compelling social reason for the prohibition of such manipulation:

> To pursue the practical possibility of genetically manipulating man is to threaten and encroach upon this free area. For it offers incalculable opportunities of man's manipulation—reaching to the very roots of his existence—*by organized society*, i.e., the state.[92]

Although Rahner argues that the danger of misusing a new possibility may be taken into account if the new possibility is justified, he does not seem too sure about the possibility of such justification. "What is the point of genetic manipulation if not to extend the state's area of control and thus to diminish, instead of to increase, man's sphere of freedom?"[93] He then argues that since the new possibilities can be discovered faster than their effects on humanity can be ascertained, "it is so vital for humanity to develop a resistance to the fascination of novel possibilities."[94] Such a significant analysis comes from both the reality of the fall and the limit on our capacity for self-creation—the givenness of our own nature.

Häring presents his comments on genetic engineering in the context of the wider theme of the ethics of manipulation. In his view, the ethics of manipulation—the use of someone or something—is set by the worldview of its users, by a technological view, or by a view of wisdom that includes "the ability to reciprocate genuine love."[95] Thus for Häring the problem is not manipulation per se: "The evil is in the transgression of the limits posed by human freedom and dignity."[96] Therefore the creation of a pure technocrat—*homo faber*—"is formed to the detriment of *homo sapiens*, the discerning and loving person."[97] Another dimension of his critique is that "behind many individual acts of manipulation that degrade the freedom and dignity of persons stands the ideology that equates technical progress with human progress."[98] So although the individual that Häring calls "technological man" is legitimately a manipulator and indeed has a right and duty to manipulate for the benefit of humanity, this individual "is a slave to ideology if he measures everything by criteria appropriate only to the field of technology."[99]

Related to the previously discussed perspectives on freedom is the concept of stewardship. Häring interprets stewardship in light of the human's noblest vocation: the capacity to "freely interfere with and manipulate the function of his *bios* (biological life) and psyche in so far as this does not degrade him or diminish his or his fellowmen's dignity and freedom."[100] Both nature and the person's own nature call "for his free stewardship, his creative co-operation with the divine artist."[101] Thus for Häring we are, under

God, our own providence and have a right and duty to plan our future and direct evolution. But in doing this, our first concern should be "to explore the true dimensions of freedom and never to take the risk of diminishing or losing our own freedom or jeopardizing the freedom of others."[102] In planning a particular manipulation, we need to think of both the means and the end. "If a concrete form of manipulation violates the basic values of respect for human freedom and dignity, or other equally high values, then the hoped-for consequences cannot justify the means."[103] This need to evaluate the means and the consequences comes from the fact that as humans we are unfinished and indeed live in an uneven world. "We bear in our genes, in the millions of data stored in our brains and in our environment, the burden of the sins of many generations and many people."[104]

In turning now to genetic engineering, Häring situates the ethical context this way: "For Christians, the theological themes of creation and procreation bring genetics into the field of ethics. The divine mandate to subdue the earth and to fill it includes man's mission to transform life according to his finest vision of humankind's future."[105] The main problem that Häring sees is "a one-sided technological thinking which either cannot or will not face ethical values and standards."[106] Hence the important ethical issue is what kind of person we desire:

> the highly qualified technical and perhaps emotionally and morally undeveloped man, or the human person with, perhaps, a less developed I.Q. when measured for technical capacities, but more human, more able to grow in love and to discern with wisdom what is truly love, inner freedom, generosity, and so on.[107]

McCormick begins his discussion of limitations by addressing the procedure of amniocentesis. Here, McCormick follows the framework suggested by the Catholic Hospital Association, which justifies offering amniocentesis at Catholic institutions on the basis that it will save fetal lives that would otherwise be lost. But McCormick notes that institutions must also implement a support system for the parents of problem pregnancies. If they do not, the very reason for amniocentesis disappears and the institutions themselves become "part of a system making abortion more likely."[108] Such a policy must be implemented prudently though, because it must balance respect for the fetus with respect for the conscience of the parents, as well as compassion with coercion.

Regarding the moral status of the embryo, McCormick argues that "there are significant phenomena in the preimplantation period that suggest a different evaluation of human life at this stage. . . . I do not believe that nascent life at this stage makes the same demands for protection that it does later."[109] In part, this evaluation depends on a differentiation between genetic individuation and developmental individuation. Nonetheless, while we cannot with certainty draw the conclusion that one is a person at the preimplantation stage, we could draw the conclusion that one should be treated as a person.

With regard to genetic engineering, McCormick comments on several specific interventions. He, as others, states that somatic-cell therapy—which alters the function of a defective gene—should be understood as "nothing more than an extension of medical practice in an attempt to aid victims of currently intractable diseases."[110] The relevant ethical criteria for this procedure are effectiveness and safety. With respect to enhancement genetic engineering—the attempt to produce a desired characteristic—McCormick identifies two ethical criteria: first, the possibility of the gene's affecting a nontargeted function in a healthy human; second, a shift in valuing humans not for the whole that they are but "for the *part* that we select."[111] Finally, regarding eugenic genetic engineering—systematic preferential breeding of superior individuals—McCormick observes rather pointedly, "Ethically, the matter is quite straightforward, and it is all bad."[112] What characteristics, he asks, are to be preferred and who is to decide?

McCormick proposes two criteria for evaluating genetic engineering. The first is derived from Vatican II's standard of the nature of the person and the person's acts: "Will this or that intervention (or omission, exception, policy, law) promote or undermine human persons 'integrally and adequately considered'?"[113] Second are four specific values: the sacredness of human life; the interconnection of life systems; individuality and diversity; and social responsibility and the priorities of research.[114] These values set a context for genetic engineering that forces us to look beyond a narrow calculation of individual risks and benefits and to take account, as best we can, of the context in which genes will be engineered.

On a policy level, McCormick argues against experimentation on embryos, with exceptions "allowed only after scrutiny and approval by an appropriate body."[115] Thus doubt about the status of personhood of the early embryo leaves open the possibility of the use of such an entity or its tissue in some research. One can conclude that McCormick leaves us with a carefully guarded openness to some genetic interventions.

Curran notes that a different anthropology will be a feature of a contemporary theology, one that recognizes a more open and dynamic understanding of human nature. "The genius of modern man and woman is the ability toward self-creation and self-direction."[116] But this greater sense of openness must also be balanced with a historical approach that prevents an uncritical acceptance of every new intervention as necessarily good. Also in the area of genetics, one must recognize "the existence of other responsibilities which limit one's own options and freedom."[117] Thus the new anthropology must also avoid an excessive individualism:

My contention is that the complexity and interrelatedness of human existence, plus the tremendous power that science may put into human hands, are going to call for a more communitarian and social approach to the moral problems facing our society.[118]

Curran identifies three dangers in the new genetics against which we must guard. First is a "naively optimistic outlook on human growth and progress. . . . Biology or genetics will never completely overcome inherent human limitations and sinfulness."[119] Second is the danger of equating the scientific with the human, forgetting that "the human includes much more than just science and technology."[120] A third danger stems from the success orientation of science and technology, which measures outcomes in terms of results and effects. Such an approach overlooks that "the ultimate reason for the lovability of a person does not depend on one's qualities or deeds or successes or failures."[121] In commenting on the preimplantation embryo, Curran does not speak of a person but of "truly individual human life," which, he argues, is present "two to three weeks after conception."[122] This criterion limits uses of the weeks-old embryo: "Experimentation after that time and attempts to culture embryos in vitro beyond this stage of development raise insurmountable ethical problems."[123] Curran is struggling with two competing values here: legitimate goals of science in pursuing knowledge and truth, and the value of the embryo. He is fearful that once the research and development of techniques now being perfected on preimplantation embryos is completed, "there will be demands and requests to do research on the embryo after the time of implantation."[124] Additionally, Curran is concerned about attempts to improve the gene pool; he is "totally opposed to any type of positive eugenics."[125] To prevent this, he proposes two limitations: no use of the embryo after implantation, and the limitation of IVF to fertility treatments.

JUSTIFICATIONS FOR GENETIC INTERVENTIONS

Recall that Ashley and O'Rourke begin their discussion on genetic engineering by recognizing that we are called to share in God's creative power and that we are genuine co-workers in an evolutionary process that is not complete. And because they recognize that our creativity is dependent on the brain, they clearly deem any alteration injurious to the brain "a disastrous mutilation."[126] Two criteria, however, allow interventions on other organ systems: (1) if the interventions give support to human intelligence by helping the life of the brain; and (2) if they do not suppress any of the fundamental human functions that integrate the human personality.[127]

Two general conclusions follow from this. First, genetic engineering and less radical transformations of the normal human body are permissible "if they improve rather than mutilate the basic human functions, especially as they relate to supporting human intelligence and creativity."[128] So transformations that endanger human intelligence and harm human integrity are prohibited. Second, radical experiments must be undertaken with caution and "only on the basis of existing knowledge, not with high risks to the subjects or to the gene pool."[129]

With respect specifically to genetic engineering, or genetic reconstruction, Ashley and O'Rourke are concerned to avoid a situation in which children are loved because they conform to their parents' preferences.[130] While this viewpoint critiques sex-selection technologies, it can also apply to other types of genetic intervention. And with respect to eugenic interventions, particularly producing a human according to some specific profile—for example, height, complexion, or mental abilities—Ashley and O'Rourke argue that "we would not rule it out ethically merely on the grounds that it would be usurpation of God's creative power."[131] Ethical dilemmas do arise, however, concerning "whether society has either the knowledge or the virtue to take the responsibility for creating the superior members of the race."[132] The theologians recognize that attempts to define *superior* are "so ambiguous as to be arbitrary";[133] rather than defining the term by the traits of a particular culture, then, they propose that superiority should apply to "a being with capabilities of meeting the challenges of new and unpredicted situations."[134] Such challenges will be met by genetic variability, not genetic hybridization.

Thus Ashley and O'Rourke see the improvement of humans as an exercise of "good stewardship of the share in divine creativity with which God has endowed mankind."[135] But humans need to exercise this stewardship prudently, "lest by tampering with their brains or the rest of their personalities they should undermine the freedom and intelligence upon which this creativity depends."[136]

Rahner discusses experiments with human genetic material. After distinguishing between obtaining the material and the actual experiment itself—and arguing that obtaining such material is not necessarily problematic—Rahner turns his attention to the concept of experimentation, making a significant observation. If, as the traditional view presupposes, a human being comes into existence at conception, we then have an individual who possesses rights. "*If* this is the case, such a person is no more an inconsequential passive object for experiments than the prisoners of Nazi concentration camps."[137] However, this presupposition "is exposed to positive doubt."[138] While strongly rejecting the conclusion that this doubt could reduce the fetal material to a thing, Rahner nonetheless argues that

it would be conceivable that, given a serious positive doubt about the human quality of the experimental material, the reasons in favor of experimenting might carry more weight, considered rationally, than the uncertain rights of a human being whose very existence is in doubt.[139]

Häring places his understanding of the legitimacy of genetic interventions within the context of stewardship, discussed in detail previously. With respect to particular interventions, he is fairly specific: Premarital genetic screening is highly desirable, and a premarital exchange of genetic information is a basic moral duty. Genetic surgery—if effective and if carrying no disproportionate risks—is the most moral and promising genetic intervention. But Häring finds it difficult to justify amniocentesis unless it is done with a view to therapy.

With respect to genetic engineering—the manipulation of the genome per se—Häring poses three questions:

> (1) Is mankind allowed to try, by direct gene manipulation, to improve the human species beyond the indication of therapy? (2) If so, can we offer criteria? (3) Can we have any trust that the technical man of today will approach such a daring enterprise in the right spirit?[140]

For Häring, the careful planning of constructive changes to improve the species "cannot be rejected *a priori* as being against man's nature or vocation."[141] Yet he argues that there are substantial reasons to "fear that genetic engineering could fall under the heartless rules of the market."[142] In summary, Häring argues that we have a limited right of self-modification, though "it is no easy matter to determine accurately the legitimate limits of such a new venture."[143] Initial criteria for discerning limits are human freedom, the capacity for intercommunication, and an affirmation of human wisdom, as opposed to technical intelligence only.

Häring concludes by arguing that our new capacities mandate that we make good use of our knowledge:

> To that end we all have to learn to discern better what genuine therapy and human progress mean in a perspective of human dignity and freedom. Those who belittle, ignore, or plainly deny these basic values of dignity and freedom have, willingly or unwillingly, called for the animal arising from the abyss. It is urgent, therefore, that we confront him now, before he is fully aroused. Once aroused, as history has shown, he will demand the holocaust.
>
> We need, above all, to hold fast to our sense of mystery, our capacity for admiration, for celebration, for contemplation, and for a whole-hearted common search for ultimate values.[144]

Ashley and O'Rourke also discuss genetic interventions. Agreeing with the position of many others, they argue that if the purpose of genetic interventions is individual therapy, then the only ethical issue is the proportion of probable benefit to risk. And they offer several broad conclusions about genetic interventions. First, although the importance of research involving the interaction between genotype and phenotype should be recognized, priority should be given to research on the phenotype. This could be done primarily by modifications to the environment without direct genetic interventions. Second, currently proposed methods of genetic reconstruction that involve IVF and other procedures are "ethically objectionable because they separate reproduction from its parental context and involve the production of human beings. . . . This contravenes the basic principles of ethical experimentation with human subjects."[145] Third, improving the human race by selection, cloning, or genetic reconstruction is ethically unacceptable because such practices "restrict the genetic variability important to human survival," and they too separate reproduction from its parental context.[146] Finally, if the mentioned problems can be overcome, "it will be ethically desirable to develop and use genetic methods for therapy of genetic defects in existing embryos, keeping in view the risk-benefit proportion."[147]

William F. May, who teaches at the Pope John Paul II Institute for the Family in Washington, D.C., though his views are much more restrictive than some, sees some place for genetic interventions. He is careful, for example, to reject inadequate views based on a one-sided scientism that does not take into account the moral nature and freedom of the human. Additionally, he strongly rejects the technological imperative that derives an obligation from a technical capacity. But, as do others, May recognizes the legitimacy of therapies to prevent or reduce genetic anomalies, though he clearly states that such decisions should not be made on consequentialist or utilitarian grounds.[148]

For May, experimentation on embryos and cloning, among other technologies, leads to the "voluntary self-degradation and dehumanization of the human beings involved and of the societies of which they are members."[149] Furthermore, we stand in danger of transforming the home into a laboratory, reproduction into manufacturing. Such outcomes of technological intervention or experimentation would be products and are thus depersonalized. However, despite this strong statement, May does see merit in some experiments and research, but he argues that the risks clearly need to be taken into account and that the research should be delayed until later in development so that "the genetic malady can be identified more exactly and the possibility of developing specific viruses carrying quite precise types of information in the form of DNA exists."[150]

May argues that premarital genetic counseling ought to be mandatory, for the process "need not carry as its consequence the dehumanization and depersonalization of the transmission of life from one generation to another."[151] As long as a proper vision of the human is maintained and those couples at risk of transmitting genetic diseases "extend their procreative love in other directions,"[152] such interventions can help specific individuals and couples and can help critique eugenic visions of genetics.

*   *   *

This review of positions on genetic engineering in Roman Catholicism points not to a resolution of the many issues and problems discussed but, rather, to experiences and values that are critical. It points to the issues of freedom, control, and power, and it highlights a transcendence within human nature that resists reduction to a mechanistic explanation. Both the religious hierarchy and theologians agree on the need to attend to these realities in planning genetic interventions.

Häring, for example, sees the protection of freedom as an important criterion by which to evaluate genetic interventions, for it is freedom that distinguishes humans from lower animals and it is freedom that lies at the core of human nature. Rahner shares this perspective by understanding humans as freedom events, as self-creating beings. As such, controversial experiences are important to face because they open the possibility not only of human choice, but also of choosing based on the value or goodness of the object of choice; that is, choice reflects not only a capacity to opt for one thing over another, but also an act of valuing, of sizing up the options, of creating an implicit prioritization. So although freedom as the capacity to choose is important in itself, freedom as the capacity to evaluate or appreciate is more normative.

Such capacities reveal a dimension of enduring worth in human nature. Rather than function according to a program or by instinct, we experience a radical freedom at the core of our nature. For Häring, this is a dimension of life to be protected, yet it is also a fundamental capacity that can lead to a more profound evolution of human nature. Thus freedom personalizes evolution and helps reveal its hidden possibilities.

Is there a way to ground an evaluation of genetic interventions without foreclosing the rich possibilities and benefits contained in the new genetics? Rahner suggests that while we are to become what we can be, we have not called ourselves into existence and we do not work with material or realities of our own making or creation. At our very center is a fundamental givenness of ourselves as created, as finite. This grounds the reality of our being co-creators, not creators. That is, we do not have final and ultimate disposal over creation, over evolution, over history. Thus a dimension of stewardship is the acceptance of finitude and the recognition that, though free and created by a generous God, we are at liberty neither to defile nature nor to confine it narrowly to our image and likeness.

Häring affirms the need to look at the history of sin and to remember what happens when the values of freedom and dignity are ignored. The history of the U.S. eugenics movement would be a good example for Americans, for that history reveals a very dark side of our society with respect to the treatment of both groups and individuals. An even more specific example is the point raised by O'Rourke and Ashley when they suggest that prenatal diagnosis may be leading us to a situation in which children are loved not because of who they are but because they manifest their parents' preferences. Such warnings about the possible objectification of both parenthood and children are reinforced by Keenan's arguments about the tendency of genetic engineering to objectify the body and to neglect its disposition for subjectivity.

Overall, the Catholic perspective tends to be conservative in its approach to genetics. The main reason for this, particularly in the official teachings of Catholicism, is its reliance on an understanding of natural law that is ahistorical and physicalist in its orientation. This perspective typically understands the stewardship orientation from the book of *Genesis* as mainly a task of maintaining the status quo and is typically conservative on issues of intervention, though not totally opposed to them. Even more contemporary authors, although they take a different methodological position in discussing these problems, typically present their analyses as a response to the perspective and critiques of official Catholic teachings. So although their framework has changed, the problems and frame of reference are quite similar.

Another dimension of the Catholic perspective, exemplified by all the authors surveyed, is a focus on the personal. Impacts or implications for animals or the environment, for example, are not major issues in Catholic analyses. In part this can be explained by Catholicism's traditional ethic that sees animals at the service of humans; therefore the key ethical issue with respect to animals is humane treatment. Only recently has the environment begun to show up as a significant moral issue in Catholic social thought. Most of the analyses of issues in genetics have simply proceeded without consideration of possible environmental consequences.

Yet it is important, I think, to separate this tradition's concerns from the view of human nature and from the moral theory, both of which support these concerns. There is, for instance, an overarching wisdom in the Catholic tradition that argues for the dignity of the person, a suspicion about power and control, and a recognition that physical interventions—whether medical or social—touch a person and not only that person's body. That wisdom stands independently of any of the specific claims and arguments of the magisterium or the theologians. Such wisdom needs a hearing.

NOTES

1. Research for the material in this chapter was supported by "Theological Questions Raised by the Human Genome Initiative," sponsored by the Center for Theology and the Natural Sciences at the Graduate Theological Union, Berkeley, California; NIH grant HG00487. A longer version of this chapter appears in *Genes, Religion, and Society: Theological and Ethical Questions Raised by the HGP* (New Haven, CT: Yale University Press, forthcoming); sections are reprinted with permission.
2. Pope Pius XII, "Allocution to Midwives," 29 October 1951, in *The Human Body*, ed. The Monks of Solesmes (Boston: The Daughters of St. Paul, 1960), 10.
3. Pope Pius XII, "Allocution to the Italian Medical-Biological Union of St. Luke," 12 November 1944, in *The Human Body*, 54.
4. Pope Pius XII, "Allocution to the First International Congress of Histopathology," 13 September 1952, in *The Human Body*, 199.
5. Vatican Council II, *Gaudium et Spes*, in *Renewing the Earth: Catholic Documents on Peace, Justice, and Liberation*, ed. David O'Brien and Thomas A. Shannon (New York: Image Books, 1977), 207.
6. Ibid., 208.
7. Karol Wojtyla, *Love and Responsibility*, trans. H. T. Willetts (New York: Farrar, Straus, and Giroux, 1981), 246.
8. Ibid.
9. Ibid., 247.
10. Ibid., 246.
11. Ibid., 56.
12. Ibid., 56–7.
13. Ibid., 25.
14. Karl Rahner, "Experiment: Man," *Theology Digest* (February 1968): 61.
15. Ibid., p. 62.
16. Ibid.
17. Ibid., 67.
18. Ibid., 65.
19. Ibid., 63.
20. Karl Rahner, "The Problem of Genetic Manipulation," *Theological Investigations*, vol. 9 (New York: Seabury Press, 1975), 230.
21. Ibid., 243.
22. Ibid.
23. Ibid., 244.
24. Ibid.
25. Ibid., 245.
26. Ibid.
27. Ibid., 250.
28. Bernard Häring, *The Ethics of Manipulation* (New York: Seabury Press, 1975), 50.
29. Ibid., 51.
30. Ibid., 52.
31. Ibid.
32. Ibid., 57.
33. Ibid., 60.
34. Richard A. McCormick, *Health and Medicine in the Catholic Tradition* (New York: Crossroad, 1984), 51ff.
35. Ibid., 53.

36. Ibid., 54.
37. Ibid.
38. Ibid., 57.
39. Ibid., 58.
40. Charles E. Curran, "A Methodological Overview of Fundamental Moral Theology," in Charles E. Curran, *Moral Theology: A Continuing Quest* (Notre Dame, IN: University of Notre Dame Press, 1982), 38.
41. Ibid., 42.
42. Ibid., 44.
43. Ibid., 47–8.
44. Ibid., 50.
45. Ibid., 51.
46. Ibid.
47. Benedict Ashley and Kevin O'Rourke, *Health Care Ethics: A Theological Analysis*, 2nd ed. (St. Louis, MO: Catholic Health Association of the United States, 1982), 306.
48. Ibid.
49. Ibid.
50. Ibid.
51. Ibid., 307.
52. James F. Keenan, S.J., "What Is Morally New in Genetic Engineering?" *Human Gene Therapy* 1 (1990): 289–98.
53. James F. Keenan, S.J., "Genetic Research and the Elusive Body," in *Embodiment, Morality, and Medicine*, ed. L. S. Cahill and M. A. Farley (The Netherlands: Kluwer Academic Publishers, 1995), 69.
54. Ibid., 63.
55. Ibid., 70.
56. Ibid.
57. Ibid.
58. Pope Pius XII, "Allocution to Those Attending the 'Primum Symposium Geneticae Medicae,'" 7 September 1953, in *The Human Body*, 260.
59. Vatican Council II, *Gaudium et Spes*, 209.
60. Ibid.
61. Ibid.
62. Ibid.
63. Ibid., 229.
64. Ibid.
65. Ibid.
66. Pope Paul VI, *Humanae Vitae*, no. 9; ed. Robert G. Hoyt. (Kansas City: MO: *The National Catholic Reporter*, 1986), 121.
67. Ibid.
68. Ibid., no. 12, 123.
69. Ibid.
70. Ibid., no. 13, 124.
71. Ibid., no. 17, 128.
72. Wojtyla, *Love and Responsibility*, 56.
73. Ibid., 51.
74. Ibid., 66.
75. Pope John Paul II, *Familiaris Consortio*, no. 32 (New York: St. Paul Editions, 1981), 51.
76. Ibid., no. 30, 49.

77. Pope John Paul II, "Biological Experimentation," 23 October 1982, in *The Pope Speaks* 23 (1983): 75.
78. Congregation for the Doctrine of the Faith, *Donum Vitae*, no. 3, in Thomas A. Shannon and Lisa S. Cahill, *Religion and Artificial Reproduction* (New York: Crossroad, 1988), 144.
79. Ibid., Introduction, no. 5, 147.
80. Ibid.
81. Ibid., Introduction, no. 3, 144.
82. Ibid., no. I, 4, 161.
83. Ibid., no. I, 4, 163.
84. Ibid.
85. Ibid., no. I, 2, 149.
86. Ibid., no. I, 2, 150.
87. Ibid., no. I, 3, 151.
88. Ibid., no. I, 4, 153.
89. Ibid.
90. Ibid., no. I, 6, 154.
91. Rahner, "Genetic Manipulation," 246.
92. Ibid., 248.
93. Ibid., 248–9.
94. Ibid., 249.
95. Häring, *Manipulation*, 4.
96. Ibid., 11.
97. Ibid., 17.
98. Ibid., 28.
99. Ibid., 39.
100. Ibid., 70.
101. Ibid.
102. Ibid., 71.
103. Ibid., 72.
104. Ibid., 76.
105. Ibid., 161.
106. Ibid., 163.
107. Ibid., 170.
108. McCormick, *Health*, 141.
109. Richard A. McCormick, "The Ethics of Reproductive Technology," in *The Critical Calling: Reflections on Moral Dilemmas Since Vatican II* (Washington, DC: Georgetown University Press, 1989), 344.
110. Richard A. McCormick, "Genetic Technology and Our Common Future," in *The Critical Calling*, 266.
111. Ibid.
112. Ibid., 267.
113. Ibid.
114. Ibid., 268.
115. McCormick, "Reproductive Technology," 345.
116. Charles E. Curran, "Genetics and the Human Future," in Charles E. Curran, *Issues in Sexual and Medical Ethics* (Notre Dame, IN: University of Notre Dame Press, 1987), 112.
117. Ibid., 117.
118. Ibid., 119.

119. Ibid., 124.
120. Ibid., 127.
121. Ibid., 129.
122. Charles E. Curran, "In Vitro Fertilization and Embryo Transfer," in Curran, *Moral Theology*, 124, 125.
123. Ibid.
124. Ibid., 130.
125. Ibid.
126. Ashley and O'Rourke, *Health Care Ethics*, 307.
127. Ibid.
128. Ibid.
129. Ibid., 308.
130. Ibid., 324.
131. Ibid., 325.
132. Ibid.
133. Ibid.
134. Ibid.
135. Ibid., 327.
136. Ibid.
137. Rahner, "Genetic Manipulation," 236.
138. Ibid.
139. Ibid.
140. Häring, *Manipulation*, 183.
141. Ibid., 184.
142. Ibid., 185.
143. Ibid.
144. Ibid., 211.
145. Ashley and O'Rourke, *Health Care Ethics*, 326.
146. Ibid.
147. Ibid.
148. William F. May, "Biomedical Technologies and Ethics," *Chicago Studies* 11 (1972): 245–9.
149. Ibid., 254.
150. Ibid., 255.
151. Ibid., 256.
152. Ibid.

S i x

PROTESTANT PERSPECTIVES ON GENETIC ENGINEERING

THIS CHAPTER HAS A twofold focus. First, I will review statements on genetic engineering from various Protestant Christian organizations and denominations. Because of the large number of these denominations, this section will be representative, not comprehensive. Second, I will present the perspective of various Protestant Christian theologians. As in the previous chapter, I will organize this material around common themes: theological anthropology, ethical concerns, limitations on interventions, responsible use of genetics, and the social issues of patenting and ecology.

THEOLOGICAL ANTHROPOLOGY

In 1989, the United Methodist Church (UMC) appointed a task force to develop a report on the new genetics, which was presented at its 1991 general conference. The following summary is based on this report and may not reflect actual UMC policy.

The report begins with five theological affirmations: All creation belongs to God the Creator; human beings are stewards of creation; technology is in service to humanity and God; there exists the critical triad of creation, redemption, and salvation; and God reigns over all creatures. These affirmations lay the groundwork for such specific values as the goodness of creation, dignity and the use of knowledge in conjunction with accountability to God, the equality of all, and "the vision of God's new heaven and new earth and the recognition of our limits which must inform and shape our role as stewards of earth and life in the emerging age of genetics."[1] How we will approach the topic of genetic engineering in this chapter is thus informed by a very clear theological perspective.

The Orthodox Church, though not a division of the Protestant Church, has made no specific pronouncements on genetic engineering. However, Father Stanley Harakas, one of its U.S. spokespersons and one of the leaders in developing bioethics in the Orthodox community, offers a theological framework and some ethical guidelines in *For the Health of Body and Soul*.[2] Orthodoxy sees the "*humanum* of our existence a[s] both a given and a potential."[3] The given is what is traditionally referred to as the image of God in the human: the intellect, emotion, ethical judgment, and self-determination. The potential dimension is referred to as *theosis*: "to realize our full human potential."[4] Thus while Orthodoxy offers an image of human nature, human capacity is not restricted by that nature. "The 'image' provides a firm foundation for ethical reasoning. The 'likeness' prohibits the absolutizing of any rule, law, or formulation."[5] Additionally, "God's energies are present in every human experience," and to speak of divine energy is "to speak of God's actions in relation to the created world."[6] Such divine energies do not coerce humans or force specific behaviors: "Fulfilled humanity—which is the divination of human life—must be free, since God is free."[7] This grounds the basis for human self-determination and responsibility. God is seen as the creator of the whole human, that is, of body and soul. Eastern Orthodoxy holds a "serious psychosomatic unity of human life."[8] So in thinking through various genetic interventions, Orthodoxy provides a very clear foundation for such reasoning.

The late Paul Ramsey was one of the early and major contributors to the developing field of bioethics during his career as a professor of theological ethics at Princeton University. He was seldom at a loss for words and developed positions that were both clear and firmly held. One always knew where Ramsey stood on any issue. In 1970, he wrote his major statement on genetic engineering, *Fabricated Man: The Ethics of Genetic Control*.[9] The positions enunciated here were not abandoned in the light of developments in genetics; if anything, he held them more firmly. Although close to thirty years old, *Fabricated Man* remains Ramsey's final word on genetic engineering, as well as an interesting theological evaluation of the technology.

Ramsey brings several presuppositions to his analysis of genetic engineering. One is that "men and women are created in covenant, to covenant, and for covenant. Creation is *toward* the love of Christ."[10] In part this means that we are created in a relationship and in part that our procreation—neither production nor reproduction—is in a relationship. For Ramsey, we cannot "put entirely asunder what God joined together in the covenant of the generations of mankind."[11] We cannot separate the good of love from the good of reproduction and remain faithful to the Christian vision of the marital covenant.

[Thus to] put radically asunder what God joined together in parenthood when He made love procreative, to procreate from beyond the sphere of love (AID [artificial insemination by donor], for example, or making human life in a test-tube), or to posit acts of sexual love beyond the sphere of responsible procreation (by definition, marriage), means a refusal of the image of God's creation in our own.[12]

Another critical theme for Ramsey is a critique of dualism. He says, for example, that the Christian will "regard man as the body of his soul as well as the soul of his body, and he is not apt to locate the *humanum* of man in thought or freedom alone."[13] This orientation leads Ramsey to emphasize the "one-flesh" dimension of marriage and parentage. He speaks of a unity of the vocations of the soul and the body and highlights the Judeo-Christian belief that "affirm[s] the biological to be *assumed into* the personal and in some ultimate sense believe[s] there is a linkage between the love-making and the life-giving 'dimensions' of the one-flesh unity of ours."[14] The bodily dimension of the human cannot be partitioned off and treated as an independent or isolated reality. Such attempts will lead to our destruction.

> When the transmission of life has been debiologized, human parenthood as a created covenant of life is placed under massive assault and men and women will no longer be who they are. Mankind will no longer be, for man is no more nor less than *sarx* (flesh) plus the Spirit of God brooding over the waters.[15]

As we will see later, this perspective has critical implications for Ramsey with respect to genetic interventions.

D. Gareth Jones, professor of anatomy at the University of Otago, New Zealand, is an Evangelical Christian who takes seriously both science and religion. In his book *Brave New People*, Jones builds a constructive framework that I will sketch out here.[16]

Jones's Christian perspective affirms two fundamental starting points. The first is that we are creaturely beings; the second, flowing from the first, is that we are always subject to God. Our subjection is an inherent limit and is based on our having been created.[17] Jones also acknowledges that we are part of the natural world and "must live in dialogue with the remainder of nature."[18] We have been created in the image of God as well as being "created to relate in fellowship to God and to share in friendship with other human beings."[19] Finally, through sin, these relations have been harmed, but they have also been restored through our redemption. Yet Jones urges that we keep in mind that "we are anomalies in God's creation, in that we are like him and yet we want to live as though he does not exist."[20] The conclusion Jones draws from this is that, to some degree, "we shall always misuse the possibilities opened by biomedical technology."[21] Similar to Ramsey, Jones adds a theological cautionary note to a field generally characterized by optimism.

A professor of theology at the Memphis Theological Seminary, Ronald Cole-Turner has been concentrating on the role of genes, genetic disease, and healing in relation to traditional Christian themes, particularly those of creation and redemption. He develops these ideas in his book *The New Genesis: Theology and the Genetic Revolution.*[22] Cole-Turner argues that we need to distinguish between the core affirmation of the tradition—(that nature is good yet disordered) and its explanation (that disorder is the result of the sin of Adam and Eve and the fallen angels). Cole-Turner suggests that such an explanation "is not needed by contemporary Christian theology or for our argument."[23] He therefore wants to retain the core affirmation, but develop a new explanation for it. Cole-Turner argues that "the earth is not exactly what God intends it to be, nor is it the home God intends for human beings."[24] The sin of Adam and Eve affected nature, and nature in turn affected all of humanity. "Since we are part of nature, our own nature is affected, almost as a genetic defect."[25]

Cole-Turner continues by arguing that modern genetics has given us what other theologians lacked:

> an empirical basis for understanding the heritability of human disorder. Genetics research indicates that we all inherit genetic defects that affect our physical and personal qualities. In a very general way, this supports the traditional theological notion of the disordered self.[26]

ETHICAL CONCERNS

The second critical theme we will address from the Protestant perspective is the ethical concerns about genetic engineering that are identified by the various denominations and theologians. While some of the issues presented here are related to other themes discussed later, the main focus of this section is a general ethical overview, which forms a context within which to think about genetic engineering.

Manipulating Life: Ethical Issues in Genetic Engineering, the 1982 document of the World Council of Churches (WCC), identifies a number of social issues relating to the new genetics. First, given the experience of eugenic movements, the WCC proposes that we ask: "What human purposes and desires does it [genetic intervention] protect; whom does it benefit and whom does it hurt?"[27] Second, the WCC advises that we should not be so infatuated with new genetic capacities that we "divert attention from the need to attend to non-genetic diseases, to protect human genes from avoidable damage, . . . and to provide each person with the opportunity to develop his or her existing capabilities."[28] Third, while the WCC recommends delaying attempts to modify various traits with a genetic foundation, it does support public discussion on the "wisdom of allocating resources to the acquisition of the requisite knowledge."[29] A fourth issue is the recognition that though a technology may be inadequately developed, there might be "no legal barrier to its use by individuals."[30] Therefore, quality control and the honest presentation of potential benefits must be strongly encouraged. Lastly, recognizing the need to be deliberate about funding research, the WCC notes that as research becomes more advanced, funding more expensive, and the distributions of benefits more complex, allocation decisions become proportionately more difficult.

Another WCC document, *Biotechnology: Its Challenges to the Churches and the World* (1989), revisits many of the issues identified seven years earlier. What is distinctive here, however, is the inclusion of a set of theological presuppositions that serve as the very general context in which these issues are to be evaluated. Three critical values are identified. The WCC says God wills a world "where justice will flow down like a mighty stream," "a world which is filled with the peace of Christ," and "a world which nurtures the integrity of all creation."[31] These values are used to develop a general perspective on biotechnology. For example, justice is denied if

> biotechnology is utilized to increase the control of the rich nations and groups over the common biological resources of the creation; . . . if biotechnology becomes a tool for genetic discrimination; . . . if biotechnology imposes on women dangerous and exploitive reproductive techniques.[32]

The WCC argues that the integrity of creation is damaged if biotechnology is "utilized by commercial pressures to manufacture new life forms that are valued only as economic commodities."[33] The council recognizes that biotechnology can help us discover and appreciate the beauties of nature and enhance the healing arts. Yet these capacities require a commitment to the integrity of creation. "Upholding this integrity, establishing justice, and furthering peace must be understood as the purpose which shaped the forms and uses of biotechnology."[34] The WCC says that the temptation offered us is to redesign the world according to a technocratic and industrial vision of creation rather than "to reaffirm the sacredness and essential goodness of God's creation."[35]

Another report, *Genetic Science for Human Benefit*, was issued by the National Council of Churches (NCC) in the United States in 1986. The motivation for this report was the conviction that to love God with one's mind "implies a serious regard for new insights into God's creation,"[36] while the love of one's neighbor requires "attention to a scientific and social movement that affects the lives of very many."[37] The NCC further says that while its voice in discussions of the new genetics should be modest and restrained, its appreciation for scientific achievement should not be unconditional, for "it is tempered always by humane and ethical considerations, and by awareness that all human endeavor is limited and flawed."[38]

Genetic Science for Human Benefit starts by identifying six areas of the new genetics that bear directly on human life: genetic counseling, antenatal diagnosis, pharmaceuticals, gene therapy, the gene pool, and assisted reproduction. The document then identifies three areas of genetic engineering of other life-forms that affect human well-being: animals bred for food, agrigenetics, and the ecological impact of genetic technology. Each of these sections presents a brief overview of various technologies and their impact or implications.

The latter sections of this document look to an ethical analysis of several major areas of concern. First is the impact of the commercial interests that drive the research agenda, together with the secrecy that such competition engenders. This can erode "the tradition of openness, cooperation, and publication in journals."[39] Additionally, the fact that many university-based researchers are also stockholders in biotech companies can create a conflict of interest. A second concern is that many recipients of federal grant money can now receive significant profits on their discoveries. What is the obligation to the public with respect to these profits? Public funding suggests public regulation. While there is an appropriate tradition of scientific self-regulation, the new technologies and their implications nonetheless call for at least a rethinking of the regulatory issues. Third, the NCC considers the implications of the new genetics for military uses, particularly biochemical warfare. The NCC concludes that whether such weapons are offensive or defensive, "their hazardous and repugnant nature is self-evident, and the morality of their being used is highly questionable."[40]

Next, the document looks to the global implications of the new genetics and raises two concerns: that the embargo of genetic information based on economic competition could have a divisive effect and that the testing of various genetic technologies may occur in countries whose laws are more lax than those of the United States with respect to protecting both citizens and the environment.

Genetic Science for Human Benefit concludes with a section that considers three thematic ethical issues for evaluating genetic technologies. The first theme is the worth of life and living. This is a strong affirmation of the value of life, particularly as a creation by God. Yet the document notes that "physical life is not the absolute value, but true humanness is found in the unity of the body with the mind and spirit, constrained by love."[41] Three conclusions are drawn from this position. First, human life is not perfectible; although efforts should be made to cure diseases, we ought not to be seduced into thinking that we can be made perfect by genetic engineering. Second, efforts must be made to "preserve individuals and communities from involuntary risks to health and life."[42] This means that participation in genetic research must be voluntary and performed under stringent controls. It also suggests that genetic research should not seek to reduce human diversity. Finally, the new genetics reveals the intimate relation of humans with all creation and gives a new seriousness to "the ancient, enduring biblical requirement for men and women to care for the creation as a responsibility to God and to coming generations."[43]

The second theme consists of fairness, justice, and love. The NCC says that from these values "arise our cherished concepts of quality of worth, equal opportunity, and participatory social organization."[44] This leads to two specific conclusions. First, all people should have access to the benefits of the new genetics: Not only should the poor receive these benefits, but also "the poor must not be disproportionately put at risk by the developing and testing of therapeutic procedures and genetic products."[45] Second, justice requires that the public funding of much of genetic research be taken into account in pricing products and accruing profits from products from the biotech industry.

The third theme is responsibility to God through human activity in God's creation. Here respect for life, as well as for fairness and justice, does not require that the new genetics be abandoned but, rather, that we advance "with utmost caution, cognizant that this is a concern of all society."[46] The NCC agrees that there are limits to scientific inquiry or research: "All that can be known need not be known if in advance it clearly appears that the process for gaining such knowledge violates the sanctity of human life."[47] This is not, in the NCC's opinion, an antiscience or antiresearch statement but a recognition that the council must speak out "when the quest for new knowledge supersedes all ethical concerns."[48] To this end, the NCC recommends the establishment of a federal regulatory commission to oversee such issues. Finally, the document argues that the NCC should have a role in the public debate about the new genetics, particularly given its belief in the "distinctive place of humankind in the whole chain of life which God has created, and . . . the unity of humankind as indicative of God's purpose."[49]

At its 1987 annual conference, the Church of the Brethren issued a statement on genetic engineering. The statement opens with key theological affirmations that provide the basis for further analysis, several of which are significant for our purposes: God is the creator of life; life is a divine gift; and life has a divine purpose. The "search for truth is a continuing process involving biblical study, scientific research and prayer, as these contribute to the decision-making of the faith community."[50] The document emphasizes that the incarnation of Christ shows the importance and meaning of human existence, that humans are created in God's image, and that this life is to be lived in community and in faithfulness to God and with God's children. Additionally, the Brethren affirm that the "human mind is a gift of God and that the search for knowledge is to be encouraged."[51]

The document then addresses several areas of concern. Theologically, the document asks how "the engineering of genetic change relate[s] to our understanding of God as Creator of life."[52] Is genetic engineering a legitimate way to be a partner in fulfilling God's intentions? Ethically, the document raises a new question: "What are the ideal credentials for persons serving on committees or agencies who make decisions about genetics?"[53] Other concerns are standard: the ownership of patents; the use of technologies to relieve suffering, particularly in poorer countries; the safeguarding of the marginalized from being involuntary research subjects; and the appropriateness of tie-ins with the military for genetic research. The conference statement is also concerned with the social impacts of genetic engineering, its possible long-term effects, and its uses and applications in genetic counseling, artificial reproduction, and gene therapy.

The Church of the Brethren then makes several recommendations, many of which have to do with encouraging members of the church to become actively involved in monitoring developments in genetics both on the level of the General Board of the Church of the Brethren and also by the general membership. Suggested as well is involvement with various federal agencies and monitoring committees. The Brethren recommends using developments in genetics for the alleviation of human suffering and emphasizes the "rights of all persons to dignity, freedom, justice, love, and respect."[54] More specific recommendations include the use of genetic counseling, seeking out genetic histories by those contemplating parenthood, church members becoming informed about developments in genetics through education programs, and providing courses on these issues in colleges sponsored by the Church of the Brethren.

LIMITATIONS ON GENETIC INTERVENTIONS

The third theme we will investigate is the Protestant perspective on limitations on genetic interventions, and we will begin by returning our attention to the WCC, specifically, to the guidelines about limitations that it outlines in *Manipulating Life* and *Biotechnology*.

Generally speaking, the WCC's tone toward genetic engineering in *Manipulating Life* is a very cautionary one. Of course, at the time of its release in 1982, developments that have since occurred in many of the fields it addresses, such as biological warfare, rDNA technology, and ownership of living organs, were still only imagined possibilities, thus the document also has an air of wary anticipation.

Yet the WCC does speak directly to the limits of the use of genetics in *Biotechnology*, for by the time this statement was circulated, the WCC was equipped with sufficient knowledge of advancements in the new genetics to heighten the level of its cautionary note and to offer more restrictive recommendations. Specifically, it calls for a prohibition of genetic testing for sex selection and warns against the use of genetic testing for "involuntary social engineering"[55] and other forms of discrimination in health care, insurance, and education. It also advises a ban on experiments on the human germ line and urges "strict control on experiments involving genetically engineered somatic cells."[56] The particular point of concern here is the use of these techniques to discriminate against those labeled "defective." The report "advises governments to prohibit embryo research with any experiments, if agreed to, only under well defined conditions."[57] Overall, the WCC recognizes that the jury is still out on many issues and thus continues its policy of watchful waiting.

In regard to issues of limitations on interventions, the UMC's task force poses four general questions: (1) Is the research appropriate? (2) Is the technology available at an affordable cost? (3) Is this technology a cost-effective means of meeting the need? and (4) Do members of society have access to the technology? Additionally, the task force's report delineates areas of special concern: (1) the patenting of life-forms and access to genetic technologies; (2) genetic medicine and therapy, which is subdivided into screening/diagnosis and prevention/therapy; (3) agricultural applications of genetic research; and (4) environmental concerns: the release of new organisms into the environment, engineering nature, and the uncertainty of problems and promises. Generally, the task force argues that the technological imperative—that is, we can, therefore we must—is an insufficient justification for proceeding into genetic experimentation.

In his thinking about the possibility of genetic interventions, Ramsey distinguishes between what he calls a "serious" and a "frivolous" conscience. The person with a frivolous conscience articulates the new ethical dilemmas that must be resolved before the future overtakes us. For Ramsey, this frequently means that "we need to devise a new ethics that will provide the rationalization for doing in the future what men are bound to do because of new actions and interventions science will have made possible."[58] On the other hand, to have a serious conscience "means to say that in raising urgent ethical questions there may be some things that men should never do. The good things that men do can be made complete only by the things they refuse to do."[59] Hence it is better to not raise such questions at all unless one is open to the possibility of a refusal. Ramsey's basic position can be summarized in his oft-repeated statement: "Men ought not to play God before they learn to be men, and after they have learned to be men, they will not play God."[60]

RESPONSIBLE USE OF GENETICS

A fourth theme in Protestant thought is the responsible use of genetics in research and therapy. With respect to somatic-cell therapy, the WCC notes that many forms of such therapy are experimental and thus fall under the traditional ethical analysis of experimentation on human subjects. Because of this therapy's ability to alter human genes, the "choice to alter one gene but not another will become a matter requiring ethical justification."[61] Nevertheless, if this therapy relieves pain, then it provides a good for the patient and therefore is justified. Germ-line therapy, however, while it may also provide good for humanity, raises additional issues because it changes germ-line cells. One issue, then, when considering any type of gene therapy is whether or not there is sufficient information to make justifiable decisions. But the WCC also notes that "changes in genes that avoid the occurrence of disease are not necessarily made illicit merely because those changes also alter the genetic inheritance of future generations."[62]

Complicating the moral analysis further is the lack of a clear distinction between removing defects and improving heredity. The line between correction and enhancement becomes difficult to draw—or even to find. The WCC here notes that "values then become highly controversial,"[63] from which two recommendations follow. First, scientists have an obligation to make clear that not all traits can be genetically identified, much less changed at will. Second, there is a public obligation to discuss the desirability of such a genetic intervention. The WCC argues against genetic reductionism and the consequent view of the human as an object to be manipulated. It also states that an "increase in the means for achieving health and well-being is ethically desirable," but it simultaneously warns that "new options [should] not become new dogmas."[64] Thus freedom of choice as a basis for protection from mandatory treatments is a core ethical issue for the WCC.

The 1989 Seventeenth General Synod of the United Church of Christ (UCC) proposed several issues for discussion that are relevant to our task at hand. The document resulting from that meeting gives a quite positive context for genetic engineering by noting that it expands our understanding of creation and increases our ability to alter the natural world. "As we discover these processes and learn how to use them, we find new ways to exercise covenantal responsibility with God in the ongoing creative and redemptive work."[65] By studying genetics we can "learn more about the Creator through the wonders of the world."[66]

The UCC document "The Church and Genetic Engineering" argues that new knowledge from genetics brings new responsibilities, particularly the obligation "to use our new abilities in genetic engineering to bring healing and sustenance to people everywhere."[67] The UCC welcomes genetic engineering with caution and hopefulness and supports the development of a climate of thoughtful reflection and the formation of various guidelines and regulatory committees. Within this context, the UCC supports somatic-cell gene therapy (but not germ-line interventions); mapping the human genome; genetic screening supported by genetic counseling services; and the application of genetic engineering to agriculture, forestry, mining, and pollution control, provided there is adequate regulation and public participation in evaluating new uses. The only condemnation is any use of genetic engineering to develop biological weapons. Despite the brevity of the UCC's proposal, it touches on many thematic issues raised by other denominations, and it is interesting in that it is the most positive and optimistic of all the documents reviewed herein.

At its seventieth General Convention in 1991, the Episcopal Church issued four resolutions related to genetic engineering:

1. There is no theological or ethical objection against the production and use of medicinal materials by means of genetic manipulation for therapeutic or diagnostic purposes aimed at the prevention or alleviation of human suffering.

2. There is no theological or ethical objection against gene therapy, if proved to be effective without undue risk to the patient and if aimed at prevention or alleviation of serious suffering.

3. The benefits of the new technology should be equally available to all who need these for the prevention or alleviation of serious suffering, regardless of financial status.

4. The use of results of genetic screening of adults, newborns, and the unborn for the purpose of discrimination in employment and insurance is unacceptable.[68]

The statement focuses exclusively on the application of the new genetics to humans and does this primarily in terms of therapeutic uses. Justice is seen primarily in the context of universal accessibility to the benefits of the technology. Though narrowly focused, the statement highlights the issue of justice in a useful way.

Returning now to the UMC's 1989 task force, we will recall that it argued that the technological imperative is an insufficient justification for proceeding with genetic experimentation. However, the task force does support public funding of genetic research so that "projects not likely to be funded by private grants will receive adequate support and . . . there will be greater accountability to the public by those involved in setting the direction of genetic research."[69] Additionally, genes and genetically modified organisms ought to be held as a common resource and not exclusively controlled or patented. Moreover, the task force supports access to genetic counseling and somatic gene therapy but opposes germ-line therapy. Genetic information ought to be private, claims the UMC, which opposes the "discriminatory or manipulative use of genetic information, such as the limitation, termination, or denial of insurance or employment."[70]

The "Genetic Science Task Force Report" also supports "public involvement in initiation, evaluating, regulating and funding of agricultural research"[71] to help ensure a safe, nutritious, and affordable food supply. Such research should accrue to a broad public and should ensure "the sustainability of family farms, natural resources, and rural communities."[72] Genetic research should help maintain ecological balance and seek "to perpetuate all of God's living creations as long as possible."[73] Additionally, great care should be taken with the release of genetically engineered material into the environment. Finally, the task force recommends dialogue around ethical issues in the new genetics and the development of resources to educate various publics on genetic issues.

From an Orthodox perspective, Harakas views genetic counseling positively because it makes more precise "that which the Church has sought to do through its canon law, which prohibits marriages between closely related persons."[74] But within this framework, Orthodoxy does not support abortion as a resolution to genetic defects. Instead, genetic screenings of populations to detect carriers of genetic defects is "encouraged by Orthodox ethics, so as to provide as much information as possible to persons before marriage."[75] In general, Harakas argues that Orthodoxy tends to be conservative toward genetic issues because in them there is "a dimension of the holy . . . relating them to transcendent values and concerns."[76] He concludes that Orthodox ethics has a "pro-life bias that honors and respects the life of each person as a divine gift, which requires development and enhancement."[77]

Jones focuses on prenatal diagnosis and genetic screening programs. He argues that amniocentesis is not a neutral procedure, for it is "closely allied to induced abortion which is regarded as the therapy for the defect uncovered by amniocentesis."[78] In the absence of the possibility of abortion, Jones notes that amniocentesis would either show a disease or not. In the first case, typically little can be done about the disease. In the second case, Jones wonders if the risks justify a negative finding, even though such information may be consoling. Finally, Jones argues against the use of prenatal diagnosis for sex selection because this makes sex a disease, contributes to the social inequality between males and females, and is a trivial and morally reprehensible use of the technology with "social flippancy being accepted as a legitimate reason for destroying human life and wasting scarce medical resources."[79]

Jones further notes that any information about a disease obtained through genetic screening programs may constitute a greater burden than the disease itself, particularly when no therapy is available for it. This information is not neutral, for with the information comes the "ability to predict disease-states years ahead of the onset of symptoms [and] will bestow upon the geneticists unheard of powers."[80] Particularly problematic for Jones are the new categories of "patient" and "disease" that genetic screening technologies will bring. "The emphasis will shift from patient to *potential* patient, and from disease to disease *propensity*."[81] The issue of control is raised not only with respect to the present life of the individual, but also with respect to that individual's future. This is especially problematic when quality is understood as quality control—an optimal life achieved through modern medicine. After noting that medicine cannot deliver human happiness, Jones states that from a Christian perspective, medicine cannot solve "problems rooted in human nature."[82] In this, he does not reject quality of life assessments or suggest that they are irrelevant; rather, his perspective is that such assessments "should always be made within a framework of an overall reverence and deep concern for human life."[83] Jones articulates the issue this way:

> If our scientific and medical priorities are based on the pre-eminence of the biological, financial and human resources will be channeled in this direction to the detriment of environmental and preventative causes: hence the élitism of positive eugenics. This is not to argue that genetic defects are unimportant; rather they are to be viewed within the perspective of the individual as a whole person and not as a dismembered biological entity.[84]

James A. Nash, the executive director of the Churches' Center for Theology and Public Policy in Washington, D.C., identifies three key criteria for justifying genetic interventions for human benefit: if "the intervention can be reasonably tested and [can verify] that tolerable alternatives are not available, [if] genetic diversity is not compromised, and [if] ecosystem integrity is not endangered."[85] These qualifications are based on the recognition that the ecosystem has "its own integrity which, in the final analysis, is also the integrity of the human species as part of nature."[86] Nash therefore argues against the treatment of the ecosystem as an instrument or commodity. He argues, as well, that the principal ethical issue is control of the vast powers that genetic engineering confers upon us. Such power leads to hubris, which needs the antidote of humility. Given that our knowledge is fragmented, our ingenuity limited, and our moral character questionable, Nash states that "humility reminds us that the miracles of genetic engineering are trivial in comparison with the surrounding magnitude of evolutionary and ecological miracles, which deserve preservation."[87] Because we do not have the power to control all the uncertainties, Nash concludes that we "ought not to exercise all of the limited powers that we do have."[88]

For Deter T. Hessel, director of the Program on Ecology, Justice, and Faith in Princeton, New Jersey, the core justification for genetic interventions is appropriateness: "It has a religious-philosophical referent, and fosters ecological sensibility, constructive social purpose, appreciation for responsible scientific inquiry, and realism about human misuse of power."[89] This focus on eco-socially appropriate technology does not prohibit the development of technology or technological interventions. Rather, "it asks for deeper ethical reflection, alert to intuitive religious sensibilities about what is good and right, and for more democratic social involvement to limit or channel this qualitatively different human activity for the good of all."[90]

In his book *Ethics in an Age of Technology*, Ian Barbour, professor emeritus of religion and science at Carleton College, reviews several of the technologies available for both biotechnology and human medicine.[91] After noting, as others have, the problems and promises of the new genetics, Barbour focuses on numerous ethical and theological issues. First is how genetic technologies shape our attitudes toward disabilities. Although he recognizes that gene therapy is a noble goal, Barbour warns that we must not let this goal "lead to resentment or condescension toward people with disabilities."[92] Worth, he notes, does not depend on the absence of defect or disease. "Unconditional love and acceptance within the family and respect for persons in society must not be compromised by our efforts to eradicate genetic defects."[93]

Second, Barbour is dubious about social eugenic programs. Such programs raise problems with respect to establishing criteria and cultural biases in defining disease and defect, and they can uncritically adopt one culture's or time's ideals as normative. Though we do impose desires and expectations on others through family and educational structures as well as social programs, "genetic changes are more irreversible and long-range—and also more uncertain in their unforeseen consequences."[94] Additionally, eugenic programs are likely to "reduce genetic diversity and encourage intolerance toward differences."[95]

Third, Barbour rejects the slippery-slope argument as applied to the distinction between somatic-cell gene therapy and germ-line therapy. Because Barbour thinks that "social regulation can allow valid uses of a technique while limiting the abuses,"[96] he would allow germ-line therapy but only under three conditions:

> First, extensive studies of human *somatic-cell* therapies similar to the proposed germ-line therapy must have been conducted over a period of many years to acquire data on the indirect effects of the genetic changes. Second, the effects of similar germ-line therapy in *animals* must have been followed over a period of several generations to ensure the reliability and long-term safety of the techniques used. Third, widespread *public approval* must have been secured, since the therapy will affect unborn generations who cannot themselves give informed consent to treatment.[97]

Fourth, Barbour rejects two variants of an argument that seeks to prohibit intervening in nature. One form of the argument opposes all tampering in nature because this violates ecological integrity and rejects the position that nature knows best; the other prohibits it because divine intervention has established permanent structures that are fixed and inviolable. Barbour sees these variants as too broad and forgetful that nature evolves constantly. But he concludes that we need to be "grateful for the amazing human genetic heritage, aware of its complexity and fragility, and cautious about changing it while our knowledge is so limited."[98]

Finally, Barbour responds to the "playing God" argument. In its basic form, this argument suggests that interventions in nature usurp God's prerogatives. Barbour replies by arguing that God works through the continuing evolutionary process as well as through our contemporary lives. Because of our intelligence and creativity, we "can be coworkers with God in the fulfillment of God's purposes" and can "cooperate with God in the continuing work of creation in nature and history."[99] Nonetheless, we need to remember our sinfulness and tendency toward self-interest. Thus the religious tradition "is critical of the unbridled drive for mastery and control, and it rejects all attempts to seek technical fixes as a substitute for changes in human relationships and social institutions."[100]

Cole-Turner develops his perspective on genetic interventions from his theological framework, which poses three challenges for theology. First, rather than initially being innocent and then falling into disorder, "genetic inclinations for good and evil are acquired through the same process of genetic inheritance. Aggression and altruism evolve together."[101] Second, if we think of the self as "the coherence within the complexity of the human organism, then this coherence of the self is genetically conditioned through and through."[102] Third, genetic research will show us how much we differ from one another and will help us "to become more aware of individual variation between human persons."[103] Thus a reinterpretation of the doctrine of the fall in light of modern genetics would suggest the following:

> What it would seek to articulate and to clarify are the convictions that nature is good but morally disordered, that good and disorder are pervasive and inevitable byproducts of the evolutionary process, that a predisposition toward good and evil is genetically inheritable, and that good and disorder affect human intellect and will.[104]

Within this general context, Cole-Turner asks on what theological grounds may we regard a chromosomal aberration as a defect? If we focus on the close relation between God and nature, it is hard to see that any part of nature is contrary to God's intention. Yet "that is precisely what we must be able to conceive if we are to come to a theological understanding of genetic engineering."[105] The conclusion Cole-Turner comes to is that

> Christian theology labels a genetic anomaly a "defect" when it is linked, through scientific research, with a condition similar to those that, according

to the Gospels, Jesus acted to heal. Acting together, theology and genetic science can appropriately use the label "genetic defect" to speak of a genetic condition that is not merely painful or debilitating by human standards but is also contrary to God's intentions for the creation.[106]

Since a "genetic defect" is an anomaly from the perspective of God's intentions, that "which is defective is that which may be changed or altered. Indeed, altering it would be seen as an act of participation in the redemptive work of God."[107]

Cole-Turner concludes his analysis by arguing that genetic engineering is an extension of God's activity. By this he means the following:

- God seeks genetic change as a proper means of creative and redemptive activity.
- God works through natural processes to achieve genetic change.
- God works through humans to achieve intentional genetic change.
- The genetic engineering in which God engages, and to which our involvement should be limited, is that which is consistent with the nature and purposes of God the Creator and Redeemer, who renews the whole creation in anticipation of a new creation.[108]

SOCIAL CONCERNS

The fifth theme we will investigate is social concerns raised by genetic interventions—specifically, patenting and ecology. With respect to patenting and ownership of life-forms, the WCC's *Manipulating Life* discusses five areas of concern. First, granting patents to microorganisms with human genes that synthesize useful medical products could allow corporations "to make excessive profits out of human suffering, to sustain an unhealthy world wide dependence on pharmaceutical products, and to ignore real health needs because they offer lesser economic returns."[109] Second, because of the inherent vagueness of patent law, commercial competition could give rise to costly patent litigation that could affect the kinds of products made and the types of organizations that produce them. Third, the high degree of market competitiveness, with its accompanying commercial implications, is causing a practice of secrecy heretofore unknown in science. Fourth, although much of the research for new commercial products is publicly funded, private companies will reap the main financial benefit. Finally, the U.S. Supreme Court patenting decision *Diamond v. Chakrabarty* "rested upon a specific, highly reductive conception of life" that could destroy the distinction between living and nonliving organisms; this in turn would allow "a shift in accepted ideas as to what may be done to living things."[110]

With respect to other life-forms, the WCC "believes that animal life-forms should not be patented," "urges the swift adoption of strict international controls on the release of genetically engineered organisms into the environment," and advises reflection upon "the political evolution of biotechnology and its impact on global justice."[111]

Hessel sets his discussion of genetics in a broad ecological context. He takes as a guide James Gustafson's perspective on ethics, which responds to the question "What is God enabling and requiring us, as participants in the patterns and processes of interdependent life, to be and to do?" with the answer: "We are to relate to all others in a manner appropriate to their relations to God."[112] This leads Hessel to argue that our ethical actions are to be guided by an awareness of God's activity in the world. Because of an awareness of God's deep involvement in our ecology, "our thinking and acting are likely to become more earth-fitting."[113]

Hessel then identifies seven theological insights that he believes ought to give general guidance to the debate:

1. Faith affirms spirit, God's loving presence in nature.

2. God is directly related to and cares for other creatures.

3. God is present in and with a dynamically open, astoundingly biodiverse, and coherently indeterminate creation.

4. God covenants with human beings to establish a pattern of right relations within the community of creation.

5. Humans are accountable for the well-being of all.

6. Genesis themes of dominion and stewardship must be recast.

7. Human activity affects the future of earth's community, even though the planet's destiny is God's responsibility.[114]

These seven insights point to an organic understanding of the universe and a dynamic understanding of God's relation to it. Consequently, the "primary human vocation is to care for creation with love that seeks justice, consistent with the divine purpose."[115] This has two major implications. First,

> The normative human role is that of earthkeeper or household manager (oikonomia), to be exercised with loving attention and appropriate humility. This involves humans in the processes of continuing creation, resisting injustice, overcoming brokenness, restoring health, and offering praise for what is good.[116]

Second, a shift from an anthropocentric perspective to an ecological one is needed. For Hessel, the traditional stewardship ethic of "*venturing* and *remaking* remains problematic, considering its eco-social effects. Protection and preservation take on more ethical import."[117] Important in Hessel's perspective is the introduction of an ecological theme that follows from his vision of the human in relation to God and God's creation.

Nash discusses the new genetics within the framework of a larger ecological ethic in his book *Loving Nature: Ecological Integrity and Christian Responsibility.*[118] He begins by noting that genetics has traditionally been discussed anthropologically as a problem of biomedical ethics or in terms of agricultural benefits to humans. He argues that the ecological dimension is of critical importance because "genetic engineering is in large measure a question of the ethics of using and abusing power."[119] While Nash acknowledges the medical and agricultural benefits that can come from the new genetics, he also recognizes the environmental risks that can follow from it: the elimination of multiple genetic strains of plants and animals, a changed ecosphere, and the release of harmful organisms into the environment. These consequences point to several ethical questions.

For example, are "nonhuman species . . . simply 'machines' to be reconstructed or information bits to be reprogrammed and upgraded without controls or bounds?"[120] Here Nash means to highlight that while a variety of bans are appropriately placed on genetic interventions into humans, "the same alterations are frequently assumed as morally valid for nonhuman species."[121] So although Nash recognizes that our civilization depends on both interventions into nature and improvements of nature, he most appropriately asks in sum, "Is the whole of nature to be defined by human purposes and subject to human improvements?"[122]

*   *   *

This overview of various positions on the new genetics within Protestant denominations and among Protestant theologians reveals many concerns similar to those raised by their Catholic counterparts in Chapter 5. Three major differences stand out, however. First, the Protestant denominations and theologians frequently locate the question of genetic engineering within an ecological setting. This forces us to consider a more holistic perspective. Genetics cannot be seen as an isolated branch of science, for the effects of it hold profound social and ecological consequences, as well as personal ones. Second, the Protestant perspectives seem to be more conservative in their evaluation of genetic interventions; this may be rooted in a Reformation heritage, with its emphasis on sin and its destructive effects on human nature. Nonetheless, this focus alerts us to the darker side of human nature, reflected in many problematic applications of technology. Yet this orientation does not generally prohibit genetic interventions. Rather, it casts a very wary eye on the proceedings. Finally, there is a much greater reliance here on Scripture and scriptural themes than in the Catholic perspective. This characteristic of Protestant theology leads to developing its perspective on genetic engineering from the position of stewardship rather than of natural law. And though both approaches reach similar conclusions, the stewardship model locates responsibility for ethical decisions within the person; the natural law model, in contrast, grounds responsibility on the order in the created world.

Although many of the positions proposed in this chapter reveal a suspicion of genetic engineering, there is an approval—granted, a quite cautious one—of many possibilities presented by the new genetics, especially when these possibilities are clearly therapeutic. The overarching concern remains the many uses to which the technology can be put and the risk of yet-to-be-discovered harms, be they personal, social, or ecological.

NOTES

1. UMC, "Genetic Science Task Force Report" (Christian Social Action, January 1991), 19.
2. Stanley Harakas, *For the Health of Body and Soul* (Brookline, MA: Holy Cross Orthodox Press, 1980).
3. Ibid., 20.
4. Ibid., 21.
5. Ibid.
6. Ibid.
7. Ibid., 22.
8. Ibid., 23.
9. Paul Ramsey, *Fabricated Man: The Ethics of Genetic Control* (New Haven, CT: Yale University Press, 1970).
10. Ibid., 38.
11. Ibid., 33.
12. Ibid., 39.
13. Ibid., 36.
14. Ibid., 133.
15. Ibid., 135.
16. D. Gareth Jones, *Brave New People*, rev. ed. (Grand Rapids, MI: William B. Eerdmans Publishing Co., 1985).
17. Ibid., 8–9.
18. Ibid., 11.
19. Ibid., 17.
20. Ibid., 20.
21. Ibid.
22. Ronald Cole-Turner, *The New Genesis: Theology and the Genetic Revolution* (Louisville, KY: Westminster/John Knox Press, 1993).
23. Ibid., 84.
24. Ibid., 85.
25. Ibid.
26. Ibid., 87

27. WCC, *Manipulating Life: Ethical Issues in Genetic Engineering* (Geneva: WCC, 1982).
28. Ibid., 9.
29. Ibid.
30. Ibid.
31. WCC, *Biotechnology: Its Challenges to the Churches and the World* (Geneva: WCC, 1989), 30.
32. Ibid., 30.
33. Ibid.
34. Ibid., 30–1.
35. Ibid., 31.
36. NCC, *Genetic Science for Human Benefit* (New York: NCC, 1986), 2.
37. Ibid.
38. Ibid., 2–3.
39. Ibid., 10.
40. Ibid., 11.
41. Ibid., 12.
42. Ibid., 13.
43. Ibid.
44. Ibid., 14.
45. Ibid.
46. Ibid., 15.
47. Ibid.
48. Ibid.
49. Ibid., 16.
50. Church of the Brethren, *1987 Annual Conference Statement* (Annual Conference Minutes, Church of the Brethren, 1987), 455.
51. Ibid., 453.
52. Ibid.
53. Ibid.
54. Ibid., 456.
55. WCC, *Biotechnology*, 2.
56. Ibid.
57. Ibid.
58. Ramsey, *Fabricated Man*, 122–3.
59. Ibid., 123.
60. Ibid., 138.
61. WCC, *Manipulating Life*, 6.
62. Ibid., 7.
63. Ibid.
64. Ibid., 8.
65. UCC, "The Church and Genetic Engineering" (Fort Worth, TX: UCC, 1989), 2.
66. Ibid., 3.
67. Ibid.
68. Episcopal Church, statement from the General Convention of the Episcopal Church, July 1991.
69. UMC, "Genetic Science Task Force Report," 121.
70. Ibid., 122.
71. Ibid.
72. Ibid.

73. Ibid.
74. Harakas, *For the Health of Body and Soul*, 46–7.
75. Ibid., 47.
76. Ibid., 48.
77. Ibid.
78. Jones, *Brave New People*, 62.
79. Ibid., 63.
80. Ibid., 71.
81. Ibid.
82. Ibid., 73.
83. Ibid., 74.
84. Ibid., 76–7.
85. James A. Nash, *Loving Nature: Ecological Integrity and Christian Responsibility* (Nashville, TN: Abingdon Press, 1991).
86. Ibid.
87. Ibid., 63.
88. Ibid.
89. Deter T. Hessel, "Now That Animals Can Be Genetically Engineered: Biotechnology in Theological-Ethical Perspective," *Theology and Public Policy* 5 (summer 1993): 51.
90. Ibid., 52.
91. Ian Barbour, *Ethics in an Age of Technology*, vol. 2 of The Gifford Lectures (San Francisco: Harper, 1991).
92. Ibid., 196.
93. Ibid., 197.
94. Ibid.
95. Ibid.
96. Ibid.
97. Ibid.; Barbour notes that since these conditions are not even close to being met, germ-line therapy should be forbidden at present.
98. Ibid., 198.
99. Ibid.
100. Ibid.
101. Cole-Turner, *The New Genesis*, 88.
102. Ibid.
103. Ibid., 89.
104. Ibid.
105. Ibid., 91.
106. Ibid.
107. Ibid., 92.
108. Ibid., 109.
109. WCC, *Manipulating Life*, 18.
110. Ibid., 19.
111. WCC, *Biotechnology*, 2.
112. Quoted in Hessel, "Now That Animals Can Be Genetically Engineered," 41.
113. Ibid.
114. Ibid., 42–6.
115. Ibid., 44.
116. Ibid., 45.
117. Ibid.

118. Nash, *Loving Nature*, 59.
119. Ibid., 59.
120. Ibid., 61.
121. Ibid.
122. Ibid.

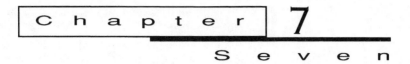

Chapter 7
Seven

THEMATIC ISSUES IN GENETIC ENGINEERING

THIS CHAPTER EXAMINES SEVERAL thematic issues in genetic engineering: the value of life, materialism, freedom, individuality, nature, and health and disease. These are important to consider in any general discussion of ethical issues in the new genetics.

The concept of the value of life is one of the more hotly debated topics in today's culture. Although this value has its divisive components, particularly when it is joined to the abortion debate, one can look at the value of life from an alternative perspective. For example, it would be difficult to imagine life having no value at all. If it had no value, one would be hard pressed to justify such efforts as the ecology movement, the animal rights movement, and human medicine. All of these are premised on the experience or intuition that life has a value, that it is worthwhile, that it makes some claims on us and our behavior. Scholars such as Daniel Maguire have argued that the value of life is the primordial ethical experience and serves as the ultimate grounding of ethics. Again, the argument is that if life were not valuable, nothing else would be either.

Many religious traditions, including the major Western religions, ground the value of life in its creation by God. Recall the majestic narrative of creation in *Genesis*, where God declares after each act of creation that what has been created is good. In this narrative humans are singled out as the only beings created in the image of God. These varying levels of goodness convey a deep value to life not only because of its divine origin, but also because of the inherent goodness of the act of creation itself. Even on a secular level, one continually encounters the sense of mystery and awe that scientists experience in the presence of life and the mysteries it contains. While many would not describe this awe as a religious experience, there is a keen appreciation and respect for the mystery before which they stand. This appreciation translates into a sense of value for life.

The value of life is further specified into an understanding of human dignity. Religiously, humans are understood to be created in the image of God. Scientifically, humans are recognized as the most complex of all creatures.

Ethically, humans experience both guilt and satisfaction consequent to their behavior. We recognize a particular moment of transcendence within ourselves and the culture we create, and this translates into an expression of respect or an appreciation of this uniqueness and these capacities. This sense of dignity grounds a set of moral obligations toward other humans and toward the social contexts in which they live. Philosophically, many ethical theories base a set of rights and duties on human dignity and argue that their actualization and enhancement is the central meaning of ethical activity.

The medieval Franciscan theologian St. Bonaventure developed a particular vision of human dignity that I find interesting, particularly in light of the conclusion he drew from it. Bonaventure grounded human dignity in terms of the location of humans within the created order and their function within that order. For Bonaventure, this meant that humans, who were created last according to the biblical narrative, are highest in the order of creation and that the function of humans is to be mediators between God and the world by representing the world before God and ensuring the participation of all of reality in redemption through our bodily nature. Additionally, human dignity comes from the reconciliation of opposites, matter and spirit, within the human being. Finally, our dignity consists in the capacity for what Bonaventure calls *deiformitas*, the infusion of grace that totally transforms and restores the tarnished image of God in humans and leads to the total fulfillment of the human in a continuous act of loving God.

This vision of human dignity allows Bonaventure to affirm humans, but not at the expense of nature; to articulate a vocation for humans, but one that is inclusive of creation; to provide a positive relation between humans and nature that can ground an ecological ethic. For Bonaventure, position is not a claim to power. Rather, position is a call to service: to God, to one's neighbor, and to nature. Position, claims Bonaventure, does not confer power; it grounds our vocation as servants of the earth. Though Bonaventure defines our dignity in relation to our place in the universe, he understands this to lead to an ethic of service in which humans are to serve as the voice of creation.

James J. Walter of Loyola University of Chicago has also identified two anthropological perspectives that help specify the implications of human dignity with respect to genetic engineering. First is the traditional stewardship model, which argues that "our role is to protect and to conserve what the divine has created. Stewardship is exercised by respecting the limits that were placed by God in the orders of biological nature and society."[1] Second is a perspective that identifies "humans as created co-creators with God in the continual unfolding of creation."[2] As opposed to the more conservative position of the stewardship model, the created co-creator model argues that "we are both utterly dependent on God for our very existence and simultaneously responsible for creating the course of human history."[3]

In putting either of these perspectives into practice, Walter cautions that we need to be continually informed by the doctrine of original sin. He recognizes that interpretations of this event have ranged from belief in the total depravity of humanity with a consequent emphasis on distrust of all human efforts to a naive optimism that forgets the sin and celebrates almost all human activity, including genetic interventions. Walter suggests a mediating position: "Though fallen, humanity remains essentially good and capable of knowing and doing the moral good with the grace of God."[4] This perspective leads to a cautious approach to gene therapy that is moderately suspicious about attempts to engineer "the human race due either to human error or to human arrogance and self-deception."[5]

Thus when we speak of the value of life and human dignity, and the implications thereof, we point to core and foundational experiences and moral intuitions that we have about ourselves and our place within the universe. Such intuitions do not necessarily argue for a position of superiority, but they do reject a reductionism that would deny any meaning of life and human existence. Such visions of human dignity also form the basis for considering various interventions into nature and ourselves.

*   *   *

Another of the thematic issues to arise in contemporary discussions of genetics is that of materialism. A specific way materialism emerges is through the question, Is the genome a sufficient explanation of human behavior? This question has been given a new popularity through E. O. Wilson's affirmative answer in his widely cited books *Sociobiology* and *On Human Nature*. The following discussion will present several of the issues he raises and critique them.

Although the term *scientific materialism* appears late in Wilson's *On Human Nature*, it is a key principle in providing the overarching framework for many of the ideas of sociobiology, "the systematic study of the biological basis of all social behavior."[6] Scientific materialism is "the view that all phenomena in the universe, including the human mind, have a material basis, are subject to the same physical laws, and can be most deeply understood by scientific analysis."[7] The core of scientific materialism is the evolutionary epic, the minimum claims of which are:

that the laws of the physical sciences are consistent with those of the biological and social sciences and can be linked in chains of causal explanation; that life and mind have a physical basis; that the world as we know it has evolved from earlier worlds obedient to the same laws; and that the visible universe today is everywhere subject to these materialist explanations.[8]

For Wilson, scientific materialism is a mythology, and "the evolutionary epic is probably the best myth we will ever have." It can be "adjusted until it comes as close to truth as the human mind is constructed to judge the truth."[9]

Of critical importance is a discussion of matter—the ultimate grounding, so to speak, of evolution. In Wilson's theory, matter is all that exists and all that is needed to account for all activity—insect or animal, private or social. For Wilson, matter is most creatively expressed in the gene, the basic unit of heredity and "a portion of the giant DNA molecule that affects the development of any trait at the most elementary biochemical level."[10] Thus we need to examine human nature through biology and the social sciences. This will lead us to an understanding of the mind "as an epiphenomenon of the neuronal machinery of the brain. That machinery is in turn the product of genetic evolution by natural selection acting on human populations for hundreds of thousands of years in their ancient environments."[11]

But is matter nothing more than inert particles interacting according to the laws of physics and/or chemistry? Does matter contain a transcendent potential or a range of possibilities that emerge or are actualized only when these particles are put into a system or when a previous system is restructured? What would be the implications of such a theory?

One response to these questions is presented by theologian Karl Rahner, who argues that we are the beings "in whom the basic tendency of matter to find itself in the spirit by self-transcendence arrives at the point where it definitely breaks through."[12] For Rahner, this means that "matter develops out of its inner being in the direction of spirit."[13] This becoming, a becoming more rather than a becoming other, must be "effected by what was there before and, on the other hand, must be the inner increase of being proper to the previously existing reality." This notion of becoming more is a genuine self-transcendence, a "transcendence into what is substantially new, i.e., the leap to a higher *nature*."[14]

While Rahner does not argue that life, consciousness, matter, and spirit are identical, he does argue that such differences do not exclude development.

> Insofar as the self-transcendence always remains present in the particular goal of its self-transcendence, and insofar as the higher order always embraces the lower as contained in it, it is clear that the lower always precedes the actual event of self-transcendence and prepares the way for it by the development of its own reality and order; it is clear that the lower always moves slowly towards the boundary line in its history which it then crosses in actual self-transcendence.[15]

For Rahner, then, the human is the "self-transcendence of living matter."[16] On the one hand, Rahner describes this as the cosmos becoming conscious of itself in the human. On the other hand, this self-transcendence of the cosmos reaches its final consummation only when the cosmos in the spiritual creature, its goal and its height, is not merely something set apart from its foundation—something created—by something which receives the ultimate self-communication of its ultimate ground itself, in that moment when this direct self-communication of God is given to the spiritual creature in what we—looking at the historical pattern of this self-communication—call grace and glory.[17]

Another presentation of matter as the ground of new potentialities is presented by Lindon Eaves and Lora Gross, who argue for a dynamic and holistic conception of matter that emphasizes the "unity of matter, life, and energy and understands nature as a profoundly complex, evolving system of intricately interdependent elements."[18] They argue for an understanding of vitality in matter that gives it depth, intensity, value, and the inclination toward organization.

Eaves and Gross operate from a biological, specifically a genetic, perspective that "seeks a new framework for its comprehension that does justice to all the so-called higher aspects of human consciousness in a phylogenetic and ontogenetic framework."[19] This perspective focuses on the mechanisms of inheritance that "have within themselves the probability of presenting new transcendent possibilities for action within history."[20] Thus they argue that surprise is inherent in nature. They develop a view of nature itself as gracious and propose, similar to Rahner, that "genetics provides *a basis for grace within the structure of life itself.*"[21] This position serves as the basis for a rejection of crude determinism, for "the material processes of life have produced a person who transcends all conventional definitions of personhood to the point where the term *freedom* is the best we have available."[22]

This gives rise to two consequences: First, recognition that "culture creates conditions for completion in community that would otherwise be impossible in a mere aggregation of individuals";[23] and second, recognition that "the conditions of life are such that the process that produces pain, in the sense of genetic disease, is also the process that maintains life in the cosmos."[24] This second point is significant in that it highlights the value of genetic diversity and provides the ground for criticizing simplistic models of genetic waste, unfitness, and disease. A similar point emerges from a consideration of the multiplicity of forms and species:

There are many forms which do not constitute a value or an advantage in the struggle of life; they are useless in this sense, and for that reason they are beautiful. Beauty is a factor that is not necessitated by lower needs, but is something that supposes the liberty of artistic creation.[25]

*   *   *

Closely related to the question of materialism is that of freedom, which is raised by the suggestion of genetic determinism and responsibility for one's actions. Again an important starting point for this discussion, contextualized by the preceding discussion of matter, is the discipline of sociobiology.

The context of scientific materialism reasserts itself in Wilson's definition of *free will*:

> To the extent that the future of objects can be foretold by an intelligence which itself has a material basis, they are determined—but only within the conceptual world of the observing intelligence. And insofar as they can make decisions of their own accord—whether or not they are determined—they possess free will.[26]

Wilson uses the example of a bee to illustrate his concept of freedom. If we were to know the properties of the bee's nervous system, its behavioral characteristics, and its personal history and then put this on a computer program, we could predict the bee's flight.

> To the circle of human observers watching the computer read-out, the future of the bee is determined to some extent. But in her own "mind" the bee, who is isolated permanently from such human knowledge, will always have free will.[27]

For Wilson, the same is true for humans, insofar as their behavior can be specified. However, because of the complexity of human behavior and technical limitations, and perhaps, the capacity of intelligence in general, such specification and prediction of human behavior is practically impossible. Wilson concludes:

> Thus because of mathematical indeterminacy and the uncertainty principle, it may be a law of nature that no nervous system is capable of acquiring enough knowledge to significantly predict the future of any other intelligent system in detail. Nor can intelligent minds gain enough self-knowledge to know their own future, capture fate, and in this sense eliminate free will.[28]

For Wilson, free will is either indeterminacy or unpredictability and is a function of a technical inability either to know all the variables or, should they be known, to program them in a meaningful way.

If freedom means a radical freedom in which a person is bound by no constraints whatsoever, then theology and philosophy would join forces with Wilson and his colleagues and argue against such a position. However, if one posits a more modest account of freedom, then sociobiology might not be able to make its case so strongly.

In the same vein, *determinism* must also be defined. Hard determinism holds a theory of universal causation that argues that there is a cause for every event and effect. From this perspective, sociobiology would argue that each of us is genetically determined and, therefore, subject to irresistible compulsions and coercions, which cause our acts. Freedom, even weakly defined, is incompatible with this account. Soft determinism similarly holds a theory of universal causation, but it locates the sources of causality in, for example, one's character or the environment. This theory gives us a set of predispositions to particular ways of acting, but it does not predict any one particular action. A modest account of freedom, then, is compatible with this "soft" understanding of determinism.

All humans possess a sense of responsibility for our actions. This is why, for example, we accept as appropriate in specific circumstances either praise or blame. To the extent that we experience an act as ours and take responsibility for its consequences, there is some affirmation of freedom. While this experience certainly would not rule out predispositions or negate the influence of one's upbringing, neither does it reject the feeling of responsibility we have for our acts. Such an experience gives meaning to our lives and again provides a foundation for ethical analysis and behavior, the basis for our quest for self-transcendence. Put existentially,

> A free choice, then, is the meaning of existence and the total initiative is left to man to rightly moderate his natural tendencies in the pursuit of being for its own sake. And in this sense one's existence is one's own responsibility and depends on one's causal initiative as an ultimate response to Being or Nothingness.[29]

Put ethically,

> Right reason also recognizes that our self-perfection, even through union with God in love, is not of supreme value. It enables man, in short, to recognize that the drive for self-perfection paradoxically must not go unbridled if it is to achieve its goal, but must be channeled lest it destroy the harmony of the universe intended by God.[30]

What is most helpful about this ethical perspective, even without the explicit religious dimension, is that while it affirms the ethical transformation of our selves, it also points out that ultimately such self-perfection is not an end in itself. To "be all that we can be," we must step beyond the confines of self and actualize that most free of all acts: an act of love or of respect for others. For only then do we find ourselves open to the depths of reality and, in this, discover our true freedom.

*   *   *

Recent discussions of cloning and embryo research have raised once again the issue of the value of the individual. In this section I will focus on the value of individuality, as well as the limits of this concept. I will address this problem from the perspective provided by John Duns Scotus, a medieval Franciscan philosopher, who is noted in particular for his writings on individuality,[31] and I do so because the position he develops is, in my judgment, a particularly helpful one for thinking through some aspects of the cloning debate.

Scotus developed what he called a concept of the *common nature*, which can help us think about the moral and political status of the genome. Scotus's definition of common nature is human nature indifferent to a particular manifestation in a specific individual. That is, the common nature is the basis of differentiating the human species from other species, but it says nothing about how or why one individual human differs from another. The common nature, in short, is our essential whatness or quiddity: our essence as a nature, what we are born to be, that which makes us human, but *not* what makes us an individual or unique.

I propose that the genome is, in effect, the biological equivalent of Scotus's philosophical concept of the common nature. The human genome is the basis on which we are human as opposed to a member of another species. The genome is the basis on which our bodies are organized in particular ways, on which we act in certain ways, on which we think in certain ways. The genome, in short, gives us a key insight into our essential whatness as members of the human species, but it has little to do with what makes us this or that particular individual.

I argue that the common nature/genome is morally normative only at the species level: It differentiates us specifically from other members of the mammalian genus. At the individual level, the common nature/genome is important insofar as it gives us an insight into our specific whatness, but this common nature has not yet been individualized, has not been expressed as a particular individual. Thus the genome, as well as the common nature, is important for developing generalizations about the nature of human nature, for insights into how we act as generic humans or what generally can bring us to fulfillment. But the common nature or the genome is not the end of the story, nor even the most important part of the story. What is significant is the instantiation or particularization of the common nature into any one individual and how this individual actuates his or her common nature. Yet how this will be done or resolved is the function of neither the common nature nor the genome; it is a function of the individual as he or she acts in freedom.[32]

I think the Scotistic concept of the common nature can help us focus our attention on what unites us rather than what might divide us. The genome is the basis for our differentiation from other species. It specifies what divides us from others, but also what unites us as a species. As such the common nature/genome reveals our essential human nature and what we have in common as a species.

Concern for the individual is also present in modern thought. One dimension of this concern is found in the dialogue between nature and the individual in Tennyson's famous poem "In Memoriam." While many of us are more familiar with the "Nature red in tooth and claw" phrase from the poem and the highly competitive view of nature that it gives us, even more interesting are later stanzas that raise a question of which takes precedence: the type, the individual, or nothing at all:

> Are God and Nature then at strife,
>   That Nature lends such evil dreams?
>   So careful of the type she seems,
> So careless of the single life; . . .
>
> 'So careful of the type?' but no.
>   From scarped cliff and quarried stone
>   She cries, 'A thousand types are gone:
> I care for nothing, all shall go.' . . .
>
> O life as futile, then, as frail!
>   O for thy voice to soothe and bless!
>   What hope of answer, or redress?
> Behind the veil, behind the veil.[33]

The unsettling thoughts suggested here are that not only does the type—or species—have priority over the individual, but that even the type may be in vain. While the latter issue may ultimately be more critical, the former will be considered more thoroughly.

Tennyson phrased the problem as the tension between nature's care for the preservation of the species as opposed to its indifference to the survival of the individual. Some, from the perspective of social Darwinism, would define this as the survival of the fittest. Others, from the perspective of sociobiology, would phrase this as the priority of DNA over the individual: The individual is DNA's way of making more DNA. But regardless of the phrasing, the vision is the same: the primacy of the species or, in a more contemporary phrase, the primacy of DNA. Individuals exist, to be sure, but their value is that of bearing DNA, of being the vehicle through which the next generation of DNA is replicated. This of course gives rise to our darkest fear: We are but a means to an impersonal end. And thus the great project of the Enlightenment—the celebration of the autonomy and independence of the individual from all constraints—is dissolved in the vast sea of DNA, "So careless of the single life."

Then too there is concern about the consequence of deriving "the" human genome. Some raise concerns that a significant outcome of the HGP will be the development of "the" profile of the human genome. The specific fear is that such a profile will be the template against which the genetic profile of each individual will be matched. This has particular significance given the development of even more sophisticated prenatal diagnostic technologies. Rather than developing a map to guide us in our search for diseases and cures, the genome will become the template against which all individuals will be measured, with genetic conformity as the outcome. Such a practice could highlight uniformity rather than individuality. Again the type would take precedence over the individual.

Scotus gives an answer to such concerns as these with his philosophical and religious perspective:

> Individuals are intended in an unqualified sense by this First One insofar as he intended something other than himself not as an end, but as something oriented to that end. Hence to communicate his goodness, as something befitting his beauty, he produces several in each species. And in those beings which are the highest and most important, it is the individual that is primarily intended by God.[34]

Thus, for Scotus, the goal or terminus of creation is not the various species, but the individuals whom God primarily intends not as a means to an end but as ends in themselves, reflective of the immensity of the beauty of God. Though the species has a place—the basis of order within the cosmos—species actually exist only insofar as matter constricts the form to eventuate in any particular individual of the species. This individual is the actual focal point of creation, and species are derived consequent to the existence of the individual. And in this vast array of individuals, Scotus argues that we catch a glimpse of the even vaster glory of the Creator.

In sum, neither the common nature (the species) nor the genome is the measure of the individual. Neither is the "gold standard" by which we reckon human worth or standing. The genome presents us with a glimpse into what Scotus would call our common nature as humans, but it is not what makes me who I am or makes you who you are.

In principle, the genome can be replicated through cloning. We now have the technology to render the common nature truly common. But what begins the individuating process of the common nature is what Scotus describes as matter's constriction of the form (what we would call the genome) to this particular individual: what we call the biological process of restriction, through which the undifferentiated cells of the preimplantation embryo become committed to the particular body part they will be. This process of biological individuation is then continued through the particular life experiences of this person. Thus the individual is the one in whom the species receives its manifestation, fulfillment, and meaning—as well as its ultimate grounding.

*   *   *

How we understand the meaning of nature is also a critical part of the whole equation of understanding the possibilities of intervention through the new genetics. The understanding of nature as a limit, for example, is based on traditional Aristotelian philosophy, which postulates an order in nature that reflects the preexistent plan in the mind of the Creator. The order of society reflects this natural order and thus incorporates the plan of God into the fabric of daily life. The philosophy of natural law, derived from this model of reality, deduces moral norms from the order of nature. Because this order of nature reflects the plan of God, it is normative and constitutes the limits of society and human action.

The traditional Roman Catholic argument against artificial contraception is based on this model of nature as a limit. In simplified form, this argument states that what nature—and hence the plan of God—unites, no one can separate. Thus the unity of sexual intercourse and procreation is inherent in the order of nature and prohibits any artificial separation of them.

Biological structures reflect metaphysical principles and therefore constitute the limits of personal and social behavior. Such a moral tradition tends to be conservative and would approve interventions into nature with caution, if not suspicion.

The perspective of nature as a model, similar to the natural law perspective above, argues that we can replicate some occurrences in nature. In this framework it might be possible to replicate certain premoral evils that occur in nature as long as one has a proportionate reason for so doing. For example, a fairly high number of zygotes are lost during the implantation process, perhaps as many as one-third or more. A number of these seem to miscarry because of structural anomalies, hormonal imbalances within the uterus, or simply a failure of many different complex systems to interact correctly. Is it moral to replicate such embryo loss in the laboratory in an attempt to fertilize eggs in vitro? Benefits to future embryos and fetuses, as well as to women unable to conceive in vivo, could then justify many research protocols. Such a protocol would be replicating a natural phenomenon in the laboratory and justifying such embryonic loss on the basis of benefits to be achieved.

This type of argument was put forward by Richard McCormick:

It is not a violation of the right to life of the zygote if it is spontaneously lost in normal sexual relations. Why is it any more so when this loss occurs as the result of an attempt to achieve a pregnancy artificially?[35]

And Rahner, basing his orientation on the doubtfulness of the personhood of the fertilized ovum, as discussed in Chapter 5, suggests that zygotes could be used as subjects of experimentation:

But it would be conceivable that, given a serious positive doubt about the human quality of the experimental material, the reasons in favor of experimenting might carry more weight, considered rationally, than the uncertain rights of a human being whose very existence is in doubt.[36]

This perspective, using nature as a model, is countered by Leon Kass, a physician and philosopher at the University of Chicago:

The natural loss of embryos in early pregnancy cannot in itself be warrant for deliberately aborting them or for invasive experimenting on them in vitro any more than still births could be a justification for newborn infanticide. There are many things that happen naturally that we ought not to do deliberately. It is curious how the same people who deny the relevance of nature as a guide for re-evaluating human interventions into human generation, and who deny that the term "unnatural" carries any ethical weight, will themselves appeal to "nature's way" when it suits their purposes.[37]

Even though Kass seems to rule out an appeal to nature as an ethical justification for IVF, he still leaves the door open by concluding that because of the goal, the unavoidable embryonic loss, and the closeness to natural procreation, "we do no more intentional or unjustified harm in the one case than in the other, and practice no disrespect."[38]

The previous two models assume that nature is relatively static. But another model of nature sees it as continually evolving. Though this does not suggest that there is no stability to nature or that there are no "laws of nature," the model does suggest that such an order or structure might not be as definitive as those in other models and that, consequently, more interventions may be justified. This view would also tend to see change or development as normative rather than exceptional. Additionally, if by "objective"—as in the objective order of nature—we mean the way nature is, then an understanding of nature as evolving is objective because such a description accurately reflects nature.

Within this model the concept of history takes on an importance lacking in the other two models. History is linear or teleological rather than cyclic or episodic. History has a future, and that future draws history forward. In Christianity, this orientation presents a dichotomy: The ultimate future transcends persons and their efforts at self-creation, but, also through their own interventions in history and nature, persons open themselves to this future and help to achieve it. As Rahner says:

> This human self-creation will develop the concrete form of human openness which leads to the absolute future that comes from God. But it is never capable by itself of bringing about this absolute future. Christianity, precisely because it is the religion of the absolute future, must simultaneously send man out to his duties in the world.[39]

We clearly have an increasing capacity to intervene into ourselves as a result of developments in genetics, psychology, and many of the behavioral sciences. Such capacities are in tension with the understandings of nature as limit and as model. Yet these same capacities are assumed by the model of nature as evolving. Indeed, one might speak of some type of obligation to intervene.

We no longer experience the past as normative, and the future assumes a greater role in defining efforts at self-creation. These capacities situate us between a static understanding of our nature and our ability to shape the very evolutionary process in which we exist. Not only is hope in our future required, but also a high degree of prudence as we journey forward.

*   *   *

A critical question raised by the possibility of increased genetic interventions is the question of what is health and what qualifies as disease. These definitions are important issues in themselves, but they are also significant because they are the basis for our decisions to intervene or not intervene.

One orientation suggests a physiological definition of health and disease. Within this context, health is functional normality. Functions are determined by design, conformity to goals pursued by the organism, and the capacity to work out its design. Each organ or system of the body has a specific range of activities, and if there is deviation from that range, there is disease. If the disease is disabling, then it is an illness.

Paul Ramsey advocated an ethical argument for intervention based on this physiological orientation, called a *medical indications policy*. Decisions to treat or not to treat, to intervene or not to intervene, should be made primarily on the basis of physiological criteria, for example, the likelihood that the treatment will benefit the patient medically. Ramsey also argued that this position leads to value-free medical decisions.

A second orientation argues that in addition to a physiological component, definitions of health contain a social and/or cultural dimension. This is particularly true in the areas of psychology and psychiatry, but such value considerations also influence how we evaluate genetic diseases or other disabilities. A broken arm, for instance, presents little difficulty in diagnosis and prognosis, as well as the modality of treatment. But when one is diagnosing mental illness, several interpretations are possible, depending as they do on one's theory of mental illness and one's social, cultural, and ethical values. While there certainly is mental illness, there is also an ideological, theoretical, and value dimension to our perception of the behaviors of those individuals who fall outside of what society perceives as normal or socially approved. Is membership in a religious cult, for example, evidence of mental illness or a sign of a deep religious commitment?

These perceptions can affect an individual with a genetic disease in a variety of ways. Take Down Syndrome as an example: There are clear physiological criteria by which one can diagnose the syndrome. There are established developmental markers by which one can gauge the severity of the syndrome and make some predictions. However, in our culture, intelligence is highly valued, and because of this, the diagnosis and prognosis are perceived differently. In addition to having a syndrome, this individual is defined as "impaired" and may be socially disvalued because of diminished capacity for abstract reasoning. Thus the prenatal diagnosis of Down Syndrome is considered by some as sufficient justification for abortion, even though the diagnosis does not necessarily indicate the range of impairment. The fact of diminished abstract reasoning is deemed sufficient justification.

Others have suggested that knowledge of an individual's genetic constitution may alter how that individual is raised. Take, for example, XYY syndrome. Some have argued that this genetic anomaly is a predictor of violent or highly aggressive behavior. If parents were to learn this, would this knowledge alter how they raise the boy? Should this boy be defined as ill, disabled, or healthy on the basis of possessing a chromosomal variation? XYY is a genetic anomaly that has a clear chromosomal basis for diagnosis. But its behavioral or social implications are unknown because little systematic research has been done to examine the effects, if any, of this anomaly. How one perceives genetic anomalies and aggressive behavior and how one thinks genes influence behavior, then, combine to have a significant impact on how the individual with such a genetic anomaly will be perceived and accepted by society. The interaction of a number of values from a variety of sources sets a context in which a physical reality is evaluated. Given that there are a number of genetic anomalies the behavior or health implications of which are not known, the problems and difficulties of genetic diagnosis are significantly complicated.

Another problematic area when discussing health versus nonhealth is the often unclear distinction between a carrier of a genetic disease and one who is afflicted by the disease, a point briefly addressed earlier. A carrier is not afflicted by the disease. Genetic screening programs identify both types of individuals. But if the distinction between them is misunderstood or confused, then carriers could, for example, be prevented from buying insurance or receiving other health care benefits because of the mistaken notion that they are unhealthy because of their carrier status. Not only may such individuals be unjustly deprived of a variety of benefits, they are also unfairly labeled as unhealthy, and this can serve as a basis for discrimination.

The point I want to stress is that the presence of built-in value frameworks influences our most basic perceptions. We see and experience in context. And whether this context is the cultural status quo, a particular ethical theory, or a definition of health, the values in this context influence what we experience and significantly shape our expectations.

These themes point to a variety of critical issues to which we must attend as we focus on specific problems in genetics. While my discussion will not resolve all our problems, I think it gives some perspectives from which to think of our new genetic possibilities. Additionally, these perspectives highlight important considerations we need to keep in the fore as we move farther into the largely uncharted land of genetic engineering.

NOTES

1. James J. Walter, "Presuppositions to Moral Judgments on Human Genetic Manipulation," *Chicago Studies* 33 (November 1994): 233.
2. Ibid., 234.
3. Ibid.
4. Ibid., 235.
5. Ibid.
6. E. O. Wilson, *Sociobiology: The Abridged Version* (Cambridge, MA: Belknap Press of Harvard University, 1980), 4.
7. E. O. Wilson, *On Human Nature* (Cambridge, MA: Harvard University Press, 1978), 221.
8. Ibid., 201.
9. Ibid.
10. Ibid., 216.
11. Ibid., 195.
12. Karl Rahner, "Christology Within an Evolutionary View," in *Theological Investigations*, trans. Karl-H. Kruger, vol. 5 (New York: Crossroad, 1983), 160.
13. Ibid., 164.
14. Ibid.
15. Ibid., 167.
16. Ibid., 168.
17. Ibid., 171.
18. Lindon Eaves and Lora Gross, "Exploring the Concept of Spirit as a Model for the God-World Relationship in the Age of Genetics," *Zygon* 27 (1992): 226.
19. Ibid., 274.

20. Ibid., 278.
21. Ibid., 274.
22. Ibid., 275.
23. Ibid., 277.
24. Ibid., 278.
25. Philotheus Boehner, O.F.M., "The Teaching of the Sciences in Catholic Colleges," (St. Bonaventure, NY: The Franciscan Institute, Franciscan Educational Conference, 1955), 157.
26. Wilson, *On Human Nature*, 171.
27. Ibid., 73.
28. Ibid., 73–4.
29. Valerius Messerich, O.F.M., "The Awareness of Causal Initiative and Existential Responsibility in the Thought of Duns Scotus," in *De Doctrina Ionnnis Duns Scoti*, vol. 2, *Problema Philosophica* (Rome: Acta Congressus Scotistici Internationalis, 1968), 631.
30. Allan B. Wolter, O.F.M., "Native Freedom of the Will as a Key to the Ethics of Scotus," in *The Philosophical Theology of John Duns Scotus*, ed. Marilyn McCord Adams (Ithaca, NY: Cornell University Press, 1990), 153.
31. See Allan Wolter's Latin text and English translation of *Duns Scotus' Early Oxford Lecture on Individuation*, available from the author in a desktop edition: Old Mission, 2201 Laguna St., Santa Barbara, CA 93105.
32. The one place where the analogy between common nature and genome breaks down is the area of sexuality, defined by the presence of the X or Y chromosome. Here I think the concept of the common nature will be *more* inclusive since one will understand the genome as either a male or a female genome. But even here I think the concept of a common nature is helpful because it looks to what is common and does not seek to establish social differentiation based on genetic differentiation.
33. Alfred Tennyson, "In Memoriam," from *In Memoriam, Maud, and Other Poems*, ed. John D. Jump (Lanham, MD: Rowman and Littlefield, 1974), LV, LVI.
34. *Ordinatio* II, d. 3, p. 1, q. 7, a. 251; English translation by Allan B. Wolter, O.F.M., *Pro manuscripto*.
35. Richard McCormick, S.J., "Notes on Moral Theology," *Theological Studies* (March 1979): 108–9.
36. Karl Rahner, "The Problem of Genetic Manipulation," *Theological Investigations*, vol. 9 (New York: Seabury Press, 1975), 236.
37. Leon Kass, "'Making Babies' Revisited," *The Public Interest* 54 (winter 1979): 41.
38. Ibid.
39. Karl Rahner, "Experiment: Man," *Theology Digest* (February 1978): 67.

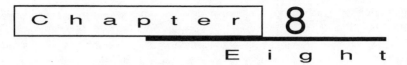

SPECIFIC PROBLEMS IN GENETIC ENGINEERING

IN THIS CHAPTER WE will look at some specific applications of the new genetics and the ethical issues they raise. The purpose is not to give a definitive resolution to these issues but, rather, to sketch out the parameters and contours of the problems.

SPECIFIC ISSUES

PRENATAL DIAGNOSIS

In Chapter 4, I described several prenatal diagnostic technologies such as amniocentesis, the use of ultrasound and fetoscopy, and preimplantation diagnosis. The result of the new genetics and the HGP in particular will be to make available much more genetic information about the developing embryo than we ever had before. The amount of information may increase and new genetic discoveries will occur; however, I think the traditional questions will remain: What are we to do with this knowledge? What does a particular anomaly mean? What are its consequences, if any? Is a cure available? Should the fetus be aborted? This last question becomes even more ethically complex when the knowledge of the implications of the anomaly are uncertain. My overall sense is that the availability of new information will further complicate, not clarify, such traditional ethical questions surrounding prenatal diagnosis.[1]

The Context of Pregnancy

The context in which pregnancy is most frequently experienced today is of critical importance for setting a tone for our discussions. For the majority of people, pregnancy is a choice. It is preceded by planning, which often includes a consideration of the partners' present family, economic, and career situations. Recent studies have indicated, for example, that the current recession is causing couples to have fewer children. Planning a pregnancy also implies a continuing commitment to the marital relationship. A pregnancy initiates a new dimension of the marriage and implies a commitment

101

to the child. Thus there is a high degree of personal, emotional, and social investment in the pregnancy.

Additionally, pregnancy may be difficult to ensure for a variety of reasons. So achieving a pregnancy may be the result of significant personal, medical, and economic investments. Such a pregnancy is clearly a desired one and one to which the couple is significantly dedicated. Finally, having established the pregnancy and deciding to continue it shows both a desire for the pregnancy and a continuing commitment to it. Thus, on at least one level, abortion has been rejected and the pregnancy is affirmed.

The Context of Genetic Counseling

Even in the current situation, with relative ignorance of the genetic causes of disease, there is a problem of information overload in genetic counseling. On the one hand, our diagnostic capacity outstrips our interpretative capacity. That is, at the present time we simply do not know the implications, if any, of many genetic variations that can be detected. Thus no clear recommendation can be made, and the couple is left confused. On the other hand, our diagnostic capacities also outstrip our therapeutic interventions. In other words, we can diagnose more anomalies than we can either cure or ameliorate. Even in the case of a diagnosis of a known and understood genetic disease, then, a couple frequently has few good choices. The range of options include: avoiding pregnancy completely, the use of IVF or AID (artificial insemination by donor), some therapeutic interventions—some of which can resolve the problem and some of which can only provide symptomatic relief—or termination of the pregnancy. Continuation of the pregnancy will lead to the birth of a child with a disorder that will follow its natural course. This may imply commitment to long-term and expensive therapy, together with a poor quality of life. In cases in which the couple chooses to continue the pregnancy, the care for the child will occur in a society that provides fewer and fewer resources.

Guilt becomes a frequent companion of the parents facing such dilemmas even though they rationally know that they have done nothing wrong. The assumption, however, is that they have indeed erred in some way. They may feel that they should have undergone genetic screening before they married even if there was no obvious reason to do so. There is cultural pressure for a couple to have a perfect child, coupled with the strong cultural rejection of the less than perfect or of those who in some fashion do not conform to cultural standards. This will contribute to the couple's feelings of guilt. They may in fact experience a sense of failure for not having "done right" by their child. Such feelings—though all acknowledge their inappropriateness and incorrectness—may contribute to an increased pressure in decision making and leave the couple with many unresolved feelings about the decision.

We also tend to assume that since the genetic counselor is trained to be objective or nondirective in presenting the findings of the diagnosis, the information provided is also value neutral. However, the findings of the screening are presented in a medical context, specifically in the context of disease or abnormality; that is, even though the genetic counselor in fact presents the information in a value-free manner, that does not mean that the information itself is value free. Since a disease is viewed as "bad," the information of its presence carries a built-in negative value tone. The information is heard in a cultural context with specific perceptions about disease and levels of social acceptability. Additionally, there are cultural, ethical, and religious standards and perceptions about abortion, quality of life, the personal and social resources available to help raise such a child, and the impact of such a child on current relationships. All these form a critical context in which the information is heard and evaluated. So though the information is relayed professionally and objectively, it is not in fact value neutral. This knowledge will of necessity present a challenge to many of the couple's beliefs and values.

The Aftermath of Counseling

As previously indicated, at present we have a limited range of available decisions, both medical and ethical, in such situations. These limitations can serve only to enhance guilt in the couple, for they may feel forced to choose an option they may not want but that is in fact the only one feasible under the circumstances. Such a decision could also impact the parents' relationship.

Furthermore, there are the already mentioned social and cultural pressures on parents. We live in a time of diminishing economic and medical resources, one in which medical insurance is undergoing significant revisions. We know that our educational resources are being strained beyond the limit, with legislatively mandated special education programs being the most expensive. And diminishing economic resources—resulting from job insecurity and the current worldwide recession—make it less likely that parents by themselves will be able to afford the major financial burden of long-term care.

Finally, we have the issue of the cultural and social evaluation of any decision the couple makes. The couple will experience a strong set of reactions no matter what their decision may be. Many do not accept that such a decision is the prerogative of the parents and seem only too happy to comment on various implications of this decision. Whether these people have any entitlement to do so is irrelevant. The fact is they do it, and this can only add to the couple's discomfort.

As we enter deeper into the mapping of the genome, our capacities for diagnosing various anomalies will only increase. But we can continue to expect a therapeutic gap for some time. Cures, therapies, and various ameliorative interventions will be difficult to develop and expensive to use. Thus many, if not all, of the issues described above will continue to press upon us.

Consequently, it is imperative that we continue to develop ethical and public policy resources that will help us address these problems.

SOMATIC VERSUS GERM-LINE THERAPY

Nelson A. Wivel, the director of the Office of Recombinant DNA Activities, and LeRoy Walters, of the Kennedy Institute of Ethics, have identified four types of genetic intervention into humans. The first two are: (1) somatic-cell gene therapy: "This type of intervention involves the correction or attempted correction of genetic defects in any of the cells of the body, with the exception of the germ or reproductive cells";[2] and (2) "the correction or prevention of genetic deficiencies through the transfer of properly functioning genes into reproductive cells."[3] These types of somatic genetic therapy are "based on the assumption that definitive treatment of genetic diseases should be possible by directing treatment to the site of the defect itself—the mutant gene."[4] The therapeutic strategy is to repair the cause of the disease—the mutant gene—so that the disease will not occur. Almost all who have commented on somatic gene therapy—scientists or ethicists—see no difference between this type of therapy and any other type of therapy performed on humans, save for the apparent distinction that the former consists of genetically engineered or genetically altered products that are introduced into the patient. Thus issues of safety come to the fore quickly. W. French Anderson notes that after the equivalent of 1,006 monkey-years and 23 patient-years of experimentation, "Side effects from the gene transfer have not been observed, pathology as a result of gene transfer has not been found, and there has never been a malignancy observed as a result of a replication-defective retroviral vector.[5] However, a malignancy was found in three monkeys, which was possibly the result of a "helper virus-contaminated retroviral vector perpetration,"[6] thus the need for continued vigilance. But this vigilance should occur within the well-established framework of research ethics within the context of the Institutional Review Board.

For Wivel and Walters, the third and fourth types of genetic interventions "involve the use of somatic cell or germ-line gene modifications, respectively, to affect selected physical and mental characteristics, with the aim of influencing such features as physical appearance or physical abilities."[7] The genetic modifications are directed toward healthy people who present no evidence of genetic disease, and "type 4 genetic intervention, if successful, could assure that the enhancement would be passed on to succeeding generations."[8] Such interventions would have to be made before fertilization occurs or very early in embryonic development. The purpose of a therapeutic intervention would be to eliminate the disease in question from occurring in future generations, rather than to treat or cure the disease on a case-by-case basis, as somatic-cell gene therapy would do. Given both the power of such an intervention and its consequences for future generations—to say nothing of the potential use of the technology for the enhancement of certain characteristics—it is not surprising that a rather substantive debate has occurred over the development and application of this specific type of genetic intervention.

Anderson has described several of the concerns: "Do infants have the right to inherit an unmanipulated genome, does the concept of informed consent have any validity for patients who do not yet exist, and at what point do we cross the line into 'playing God'?"[9] In addition to these primarily therapeutic questions, Anderson recognizes the problems that could arise if such technologies were to be used for enhancement: "We have too little understanding of what normal function is to attempt to improve on what we think is 'normal.'"[10] Thus Anderson says that to try to correct a genetic defect "that causes a serious illness is one thing, but to try to alter a characteristic such as size (by administration of a growth hormone gene to a normal child, for example) is quite another."[11]

Wivel and Walters succinctly summarize the pros and cons of the arguments:

Arguments in Favor:

- Moral obligation of health professions to use best available treatment methods;
- Parental autonomy and access to available technologies for purposes of having a healthy child;
- Germ-line gene modification more efficient and cost-effective than somatic-cell gene therapy;
- Freedom of scientific inquiry and intrinsic value of knowledge.

Arguments Against:

- Expensive intervention with limited applicability;
- Availability of alternative strategies for preventing genetic diseases;
- Unavoidable risks, irreversible mistakes;
- Inevitable pressures to use germ-line modification for enhancement.[12]

This summary represents a clear statement of the status quo in the germ-line debate. Both the research and the arguments will continue. Presently, there is neither an official public policy nor applications for germ-line modification in humans, and the argument is at a theoretical level. How the germ-line modification argument is resolved will reveal as much about state-of-the-art genetic technologies as it will about our desire to intervene in human evolution.

GENETICS AND BEHAVIOR

The New Context of the Genes/Behavior Debate

Three scientific developments are helping to increase the acceptability of findings about behavioral genetics. First is "the huge accumulation of data about hereditary influences in animal behavior."[13] These studies have been aided by a more precise understanding of how a gene affects a clearly defined behavior in a specific way. There is also a recognition that many genes, not just a single gene, cause behavioral changes. This recognition, of course, makes the search for genetic influences more difficult, but new techniques are constantly being developed to address this difficulty.[14]

Second, larger and more sophisticated studies of humans are being conducted. One such study is under the direction of Thomas J. Bouchard of the Minnesota Center for Twin and Adoption Research. For the last fifteen years, this study has focused on "almost a thousand pairs of twins, identical and fraternal, of whom 128 pairs were reared in different homes."[15] The study gives solid support to genetic influence on behavior.

The final development is "the growing understanding that the interaction of genes and environment is much more complicated than the simple 'violence genes' and 'intelligence genes' toted in the popular press."[16] This new direction recognizes the interactivity between the environment and genes.

Continuing Concerns

Although the context for understanding genes and behavior is becoming more sophisticated, a number of concerns remain. Some are technical: "misuse of statistical methods, failure to define the trait under study, bias in the selection of cases and controls, and inadequate sample sizes."[17] Additionally, psychological characteristics of humans are not distributed in the either/or dichotomies of traditional Mendelian genetics.[18] These concerns are important and must be addressed in continuing studies.

Another set of concerns, perhaps the one raised most frequently, at least in the popular press, has to do with human freedom and responsibility. Directly stated, the assumption is that if genes control our behavior, then we are not responsible for our behavior. While some have made such claims in the past, present researchers do not make such unilinear causal arguments, nor do they argue that a particular genetic abnormality has one and only one behavioral manifestation. Minimally, such a position would disregard the impact of both the physical and the social environment. Maximally, such a claim would vastly overstate the evidence. Jerome Kagan, a psychologist long involved in such studies, captures the right balance:

> Each of us does inherit a temperamental bias to one or more characteristics, but we also inherit the human capacity for restraint. Most of the time

humans are able to control the behavior that their temperaments press upon them, if they choose to do so. The new research on temperament and biology should not be used to excuse asocial behavior.[19]

The ambivalence about the interplay between genes and behavior is captured by Richard J. Herrnstein, a Harvard psychologist: "On the one hand, the conventional wisdom rushes out to embrace shaky studies that argue that alcoholism is genetically determined, but the idea that intelligence has a genetic component is pure anathema."[20] Robert Plomin of Pennsylvania State University argues that although "the role of inheritance in behavior has become widely accepted, even for sensitive domains such as IQ," some caveats remain.[21] Plomin states that "nongenetic sources of variance are important because genetic variance rarely accounts for as much as half of the variance of behavioral traits."[22] Moreover, there is the critical finding of "the absence of evidence that genetic influence on behavior is primarily due to one or two major genes. It seems more reasonable to hypothesize that many genes each with small effect are involved."[23] Or one can follow some of the ideas of evolutionary psychology, which employs a two-pronged approach to the study of human behavior. First is a study of "'species-typical mental adaptations'—also known as 'human nature.'"[24] The substantive assumption here is that there "*is* such a thing as human nature—that people everywhere have fundamentally the same minds."[25] The second approach is "respect for the power of environment."[26] Of critical importance here is that evolutionary psychologists argue that the "human mind has been designed to adjust to social circumstances."[27] What they do not argue is that such responses are determined, as an older generation of psychologists would have it. Rather, evolutionary psychologists

believe that the developmental programs that convert social experience into personality were created by natural selection, which is to say that those programs lie in our genes. Thus, to think clearly about the influence of environment we must think about what sorts of influences would have been favored by natural selection.[28]

Thus this debate will become more complex because of the sophistication of both the genetic studies and the very phrasing of the question. But a more sophisticated phrasing of the question also encourages a more sophisticated pursuit of the relation between our genetic structure and our environment, and of how both of these relate to the issue of human freedom and responsibility. Daniel J. Kevles, a historian of science at the California Institute of Technology, reminds us that "our conception of human equality, in love or in law, derives not from our biology but from our principles."[29]

General Issues

Undoubtedly the eventual mapping of the human genome will be a boon to science, medicine, and anthropology. This map will help us learn much of what makes us human and where to look for anomalies that cause disease, and it will be of great assistance in correcting those errors. We are genuinely on the edge of a new revolution in medicine, one that will provide access to the very structure of our nature. We will be able to literally reach inside ourselves, remove a gene(s), and either correct or replace it. Such power is truly awe inspiring. Yet there are dangers as well. There is talk in the air of the new genetics giving rise to a new eugenics, and there is concern that the genome will be the standard by which all are evaluated. The individual seems again to be in danger of being subordinated to the "type." Additionally, new developments in behavioral genetics are amassing convincing evidence for the role of genes in all manner of human behavior, from sexual preference to choice of political perspectives or marriage partners.

The embryo division experiment by Drs. Jerry Hall and Robert Stillman of Washington University, and the brief but lively discussion that followed it, raised once again many of the thematic issues entailed in genetic engineering: power, arrogance, the technological imperative, acting before thinking, degradation of human beings, and the violation of their unique genetic structure. The experiment also raised the importance of helping infertile couples, of learning more about the developmental process of preimplantation embryos, and of developing a cure for infertility. Public and professional reaction seemed to be quite strong against the practice. Even though the experiment was cleared by the university's research ethics committee, Stillman and Hall have retired from the embryo division business, at least for the present.

Finally, a major chapter of the cloning debate was written by Dr. Ian Wilmut of Scotland, on 22 February 1997, with his announcement that he had successfully cloned a lamb, which he named Dolly. This is the first successful example of cloning or nuclear transfer technology in a mammal. More significant, the nucleus of the cell that produced Dolly came from a six-year-old ewe.

Every cell of one's body contains all the genetic information needed to make a whole other being. Very early in embryonic development, however, this information is selectively "turned off," and various cells become committed to becoming specific body parts through a process called *restriction*. The technological breakthrough of Dolly, then, is that Dr. Wilmut succeeded, after 277 attempts, in having the DNA from a six-year-old cell "turn on" and become the source of the genetic information that led to the development of the lamb. Two elements are critical here: (1) that the DNA was in fact turned on again; and (2) that the cell was six years old. The method consisted of applying an electrical charge to the fused cell so that its contents emerged from the nucleus and the process of cell division began.

This experiment has set off yet another massive international debate on bioethical issues. Therefore, I will examine various dimensions of cloning as a way to bring together several themes previously developed in this section.

The Cultural Debate over Cloning

The Media Presentation

Many of the reports of Dolly's unique origin appeared in the economics section of newspapers. This is not unusual, for genetics news has been regularly placed in that section ever since gene companies went public in the mid-1980s. Genes are big business. Some of the reporting vacillated between praise for the technology and concern about whether ethical concerns might harm the growing biotechnical market. On the one hand, biotech leaders affirmed the immorality of full human cloning; on the other, they were concerned that the ethical concerns not rise too fast lest this rapidly growing industry be impeded, particularly in its agricultural and animal applications. Thus Dolly has raised the science/ethics debate once more, but this time the debate is being mediated by major financial interests of the biotechnical-industrial complex that is a new factor in such debates.

Another interesting perspective is shown in the comments of some senior American scientists who dismissed the significance of the research by suggesting that one could not write a grant proposal to clone a sheep because the scientific intent was unclear. Another suggested that the project was mundane and merely technological. Is this professional jealousy? Remember that the United Kingdom is now two points ahead of American science: Patrick Steptoe and Robert Edwards had the first IVF baby, and now Wilmut has the first cloned mammal. While it is true that scientists are motivated by the quest for knowledge, they are also motivated by the desire for patents and for the financial rewards that accompany them. Perhaps it was no accident that a few days after the announcement of Dolly, American scientists announced that they had cloned two rhesus monkeys, though they used embryonic cells, not the more difficult, older cells that were Dolly's progenitor.

A final story about cloning was found in the entertainment section of papers, which discussed various cloning movies. Of note was the split between how cloning has been presented as comedy or as science fiction terror stories. While the comedy *Multiplicity* did not do well at the box office, it did show some practical applications of the technology to help resolve domestic complications. And it related that sometimes when one makes a copy, the second is not quite as sharp as the first. Another comedy, *Twins*, showed the humorous possibilities of cloning by presenting identical twins who were not at all identical. Their obvious differences were blamed on making one twin from leftover materials, or what is technically referred to as "junk DNA"—the sections of DNA the functions of which we do not know. The thriller *Jurassic Park* told the familiar morality tale of the evils of commercialization of technology. The movie ended with all but the "villains," particularly the "mad scientist," living happily ever after, but much material remained to clone a sequel.

The Cultural Framing of the Debate

What I term "ethics hysteria" has dominated much media coverage. This hysteria takes the worst possible ethical, and most technically improbable, scenario and builds the case for rejecting cloning on the basis of this scenario. Probably the best single example of such a presentation of cloning was the 10 February 1997 cover of *Der Spiegel*, the German equivalent of *Time* magazine. Marching down the cover were multiple copies of Adolf Hitler, Albert Einstein, and supermodel Claudia Schiffer. While not all of the figures may represent everyone's worst-case scenarios, the technology of cloning is presented as replicating an infinite series of beings who are not only genetically identical, but exact copies of the very same person. Now, cloning indeed creates an offspring that is genetically identical to the donor of the DNA. But what follows from that? Yes, the clone is genetically identical to its source, it may even look identical; but the clone and the donor quickly begin to part ways. They are two distinct individuals, and they each have their own environment in which they are raised.

Another dimension of the cultural presentation of the cloning debate is the assumption of various forms of genetic reductionism. The argument is that by simply replicating my genetic code, I am replicated. The hidden premise is that all that I need to make me "me" is my genetic profile. Such an argument ignores the role the environment plays, to say nothing of any transcendent or personal dimensions of the human.

To understand this better, consider human identical twins, which are in fact clones of nature. The fertilized egg divides, and the result is two distinct individuals with an identical genetic profile. We know that many studies on identical twins have shown that they share many interests and similarities, even when raised apart in radically different environments. Perhaps these studies are what drive the fantasy that creating clones of Michael Jackson or Michael Jordan would create beings with exactly the same abilities and interests, perhaps even at parthenogenetic conception.

Although our genetic heritage strongly influences us, environment also plays a large role. Suppose Michael Jordan's clone were raised in an environment or a culture that did not value the career option of professional sports. Would a genetic determinism be at work that would impel him to play basketball no matter what? This is the great flaw in the cloning debate: the assumption that genetics will always override environmental influences. And that is simply not true. Nonetheless, the argument of genetic determinism or genetic reductionism is unfortunately presented as both the assumption of the outcome of cloning as well as the major argument to prohibit human cloning.

The Ethical Debate over Cloning

In the debate over cloning as it relates to humans, a distinction must be made between full human cloning—research directed to produce an adult clone—and research on cloning up to but not including implantation in a uterus. The distinction is important for two reasons. First, research on the human preimplantation embryo could be important for learning about embryonic development or for the process of reproduction. Second, different moral claims can be made about the preimplantation embryo and the individuated human embryo.

Cloning and the Preimplantation Embryo

One of the claims about cloning is that it violates individuality or the individual's right to a unique genetic identity. First, it is important to distinguish between genetic uniqueness and individuality. A preimplantation embryo is genetically unique in that it is a new combination of the genes from the mother and the father. But it is more precise to say that this preimplantation embryo represents the next genetic generation precisely because it has not yet reached the developmental stage of reduction in which the cells become irreversibly committed to forming specific body parts in a particular body. Or to say this more technically, there is as yet no differential gene expression. I argue that the pre-embryo presents the biological equivalent of Scotus's philosophical concept of the common nature, which was discussed in Chapter 7. That is, because the cells of the preimplantation embryo have the ability of totipotency, they are most properly designated as representing what is common to humanity. The genetic structure they possess is generic to the species but is not yet identified with a particular individual. Though the cells of the preimplantation embryo possess a biological, teleological unity that will eventuate into a single human being, until these cells lose the capacity for totipotency through the process of restriction and become differentially expressed, we do not have what Normond M. Ford calls an "ontological individual." Such individuality is irreversible both biologically, in that the part cannot be divided into a whole human, and philosophically, in that this being now manifests indivisibility.

In this debate, much has been made of genetic uniqueness. One argument is that genetic uniqueness is established at fertilization. Given what we know about embryogenesis, a more precise way to describe fertilization is as either the establishment of the next genetic generation or as the establishment of the common nature. That is, while it is correct that the preimplantation embryo contains the appropriate genetic information for that organism's development, that genetic information is not morally privileged through association with a specific individual. The genetic uniqueness is associated with what is common to all—human nature—not a particular individual because such an entity does not yet exist. The claim of the moral relevance of genetic uniqueness is appropriately made of the pre-embryo only after the process of restriction has occurred and we have the only individual who in fact will emerge from the constriction of the common nature to this particular individual. This is the one, all things being equal, who will become the agent of acts.

Some also argue that personhood is coincident with the formation of genetic uniqueness, which is further assumed as coincident with fertilization. In addition to the biological problems with this position that have just been described, there are philosophical problems. One is genetic reductionism: the reduction of the person to his or her genetic structure only. To identify the person with the genetic structure is to say that we are nothing more than our genes. While it is clear that our genetic structure has much to do with who we are, we are not simply the sum of our genetic code. Second, Scotus's argument about the essentiality of incommunicability as the essence of personhood is useful here. For what the preimplantation embryo precisely lacks is incommunicability, as it is biologically indifferent to singleness until after restriction occurs. Any of its individual cells until that time can be a whole other being; whereas after restriction, a liver cell will be only a liver cell, a heart cell, only a heart cell, and so on in that individual. Individuation means that a single being cannot be divided into a whole other; rather, it can be divided only into parts. Thus after restriction there is an incommunicability of the individual.

What then are we to think of research on the preimplantation embryo, either by dividing its cells or by nuclear transplantation? First, let us examine dividing the cells of the preimplantation embryo into separate entities. What one has with the preimplantation embryo is a teleologically united cluster of cells that have the capacity to become a distinct or ontological individual. The preimplantation embryo is neither all of humanity nor a particular human; it is the common nature out of which a particular, individual human can develop. Therefore, to divide the four, eight, or sixteen cells of the pre-embryo into separate cells is not, in the memorably inaccurate phrasing of Germain Grisez, "splitting themselves in half."[30] Rather, it is to divide the whole organism into its parts that themselves can become wholes. To do so is neither to divide an ontological individual nor to violate that entity's distinct individuality. Though living, a bearer of the human genome, distinct from mother and father, and the next genetic generation, the preimplantation embryo does not form the basis for a claim of an absolute value for this entity because there is as yet no subject of such a claim. There is no individual.

Second, let us consider cloning. Organism cloning, as distinct from gene and cell cloning, takes the nucleus of an adult cell and puts it in the enucleated cell of another organism. The purpose is to replicate genetically the adult organism from which the nucleus came. The key to cloning is that while each adult cell contains all the DNA necessary for the development of an entire organism, not all of that DNA is expressed. Such differential gene expression makes possible the development of the individual body parts and organs. The technical key to the success of cloning is to discover whether these unexpressed genes in the adult cell can be "turned on" and produce a genetically identical organism.

The common argument against cloning is that it violates the genetic uniqueness of the preimplantation embryo. This claim of moral standing based on genetic uniqueness of the preimplantation embryo cannot be sustained, for there is no subject of whom the claim can be made, as previously argued. Additionally, even if cloning of humans were to succeed, what is replicated is the genetic structure, not the individual. No one claims that genetically identical twins violate each other's right to genetic individuality by virtue of bearing the same genetic structure. So the more critical moral claim, in my view, is that of individuality, which is biologically secured only after restriction. Genetic uniqueness and its relation to identity are important for questions of lineage, but they are not the totality of individuality.

How does one evaluate the morality of acts performed upon the preimplantation embryo, whether obtained by division of the preimplantation embryo or by nuclear transplantation or cloning? I suggest an examination of the object, of the intention and the circumstances of the act (particularly the circumstances of the desired end result), of the way the act is performed, of the likely success of the act, and of the circumstance of place.[31]

With respect to the object—the preimplantation embryo—this entity has a premoral value in that it is living, bears the human genome, and has a biological teleology directed to the moral category of personhood. However, since there is no individual subject of whom a claim can be made, there can be no violation of individuality or personhood. This premoral value must be judged in the light of other premoral and moral goods, such as the benefits to come from research on these entities and the good of assisting in reproduction. I conclude that such benefits could outweigh the claims of protection of the pre-embryo and that research, including division of the cells of the pre-embryo and experiments to discover the mechanisms to turn unexpressed genes on, could be done on the human pre-embryo.

Considerations of the likely success of the act of cloning are difficult to calculate, for one genuinely does not know the full outcome or range of consequences that may follow the first experiment. This suggests the need to consider the intentions, as well as the end at which one aims, very carefully. If the purpose of the cloning is to learn more of early cell development to aid in IVF, one could accept a lower level of expected success because the purpose is narrow and focused on internal development of the cells. Experiments attempting to activate unexpressed genes could also be justified, even though the chances of success may be low. The end of the experiment is focused on internal mechanisms of the gene. Experiments that seek to apply such knowledge, however, would have to be very carefully examined in light of the end and the intention.

I interpret the circumstance of place to refer to the question of the priority of genetic research in relation to other priorities in health care. Because such research is so expensive and applicable to only a narrow range of cases, a strong argument can be made against such research. But if one broadens the scope of the research to include an understanding of the mechanisms of gene expression (e.g., a better understanding of the immune system), then the range of application broadens in tandem and a different moral argument can be made. What is important is that the criterion of the circumstance of place makes us look to the setting of the research and its location in the full range of health care services as an appropriate source for moral evaluation of the act we wish to undertake.

Therefore, I argue that individuality takes moral precedence over genetic uniqueness and is the key to the ethical analysis of research on the preimplantation embryo. Though I am factually the only one who bears my genetic identity, in principle, genetic identity is not unique. Genetic identity can be replicated either in vivo, through a natural cleavage of the pre-embryo into genetically identical twins, or in vitro, through division of the cells of the pre-embryo or through organismic cloning (now done on a sheep and two rhesus monkeys). My genetic identity is significant because it constitutes the establishment of my bodyliness, my human nature, and gives the basis for tracing my lineage. But more significant is individuality both in the sense of indivisibleness and in the sense of the subject of moral acts. For it is only that "I" who cannot be divided into parts, who can personalize that genetic structure, and who can transcend that genetic structure in an act of self-commitment. The absence of such individuality in the pre-embryo provides a key justification for the lack of its absolute protection, just as the presence of such individuality is a significant feature of its moral evaluation.

Thus, given an extremely careful consideration of both the moral status of the preimplantation embryo and the significance of the research involved, an argument can be made to justify genetic research up to the point at which the process of restriction occurs, approximately at two weeks. Until this time the preimplantation embryo does not have a claim to true individuality and thus lacks the full moral protection associated with personhood, which cannot occur at least until such individuality is established. The moral argument justifying such research is, in my judgment, a very narrow one and one that must be examined on a case-by-case basis and be surrounded by appropriate safeguards to prevent unwarranted extensions.

Full Human Cloning

Attempts to replicate genetic copies of individuals through full human cloning present a different moral scenario. Rather than an attempt to understand basic biological processes, full human cloning is an attempt to replicate a person with another's genetic profile. The main element in this part of the debate centers mainly on the various purposes and intentions of those individuals who desire cloning. In other words, the current arguments for full human cloning all revolve around some sort of use of human clones for the benefit of the "cloner," for want of a better term. Thus the scenarios we hear of are clones as replacements for deceased children, clones as sources for spare parts for organ transplantations, clones to perform specialized social or work functions—usually the menial ones we do not wish to do—and clones for reasons of vanity: One of a good thing is never enough.

Common to all of these arguments is the reduction of humans to means only, a rejection of the dignity of both the cloner and the cloned, and essentially the possibility of developing a market for such human clones. I am particularly concerned by this first matter—reduction of humans to means only—because of a well-publicized case several years ago. This case, though not a cloning case, strikes me as quite relevant to the full human cloning debate for two reasons: (1) It shows the degree to which we are prepared to reduce others of our kind to a means to serve our needs; and (2) it lays the groundwork for support of cloning. Specifically, several years ago a woman was dying of cancer and a bone marrow transplantation was the final therapy proposed to save her life. No matching donors had been found. The best hope for a matching donor was another sibling, but the woman was an only child. So her father underwent a reversal of his vasectomy so he and his wife could conceive a child in the hope that this child might serve as a source of blood marrow for their older daughter. There was no guarantee that the sibling would be a match, but there was a reasonable probability because of the commonality of the genetic inheritance. The reversal was successful, and the couple conceived a child who indeed proved to be a match for her older sister. Her blood marrow was taken when she was six months old, and the transplant was successful.

This is a case of creating a human being for the exclusive purpose of serving another human's needs. What is most morally problematic here is that the majority of citizens either agreed with this decision or argued that it was this couple's right to do as they pleased. The mentality that allows people to use others as means to desired ends is already in place, and this is the critical ethical problem that must be addressed in the full human cloning debate. We do need to remember that the being produced through cloning will be a human person, a distinct individual and a member of the moral community of persons. Clones are not simply genetic replacements. Such replacement talk assumes that "we" are not "they," though both are genetically identical. But such an assumption is wrong precisely because it is the "weness" of our genes in the "theyness" of their genes that we desire. How else could they be replacements for us if they were not genetically identical to us? To reduce such beings to commodities is to do the same to ourselves. Communality of genetic identity suggests communality of fate. Or to quote John Donne: Ask not "for whom the bell tolls; it tolls for thee."

There are good and valid reasons for not permitting full human cloning. The majority of them, in fact, have already been discussed in terms of reasons why we might want to clone: having replacement organs or persons, having a specialized workforce, ensuring an endless supply of performers in various areas of popular culture, and the especially vain reason of duplicating oneself on the basis of liking oneself so much. Common to many of the reasons supporting full human cloning are arguments that are crassly utilitarian and utterly self-serving. These should make us very nervous because they reveal very clearly significant class, economic, and power differences in our society. Such divisions already wreak enough havoc in our society. Why multiply them through cloning? But perhaps the best argument against human cloning was voiced by former New York governor Mario Cuomo, who revealed an extraordinary amount of wisdom in commenting: "Living with the accumulated knowledge of your imperfections, it would be hard to want to reproduce yourself and then have the arrogance to face the God who will judge you."[32]

THE HUMAN GENOME PROJECT

In Chapter 4, I gave a basic overview of the Human Genome Project. Here I wish to focus on some broader issues than the ones mentioned previously. Karen Lebacqz of the Pacific School of Religion in Berkeley raises the issue of justice with respect to the HGP. One aspect of this issue has to do with reaping the benefits of research without sharing the burdens of the cost. This was a specific concern of James Watson, former head of the HGP. Lebacqz quotes Watson as saying, "They [the Japanese] would let us pay for the basic research and they'd spend their money on commercial applications and pursuits."[33] Lebacqz questions the view of justice in this statement. Another aspect has to do with sharing the information derived from the HGP. Would this be available to all—particularly since the genome is common to the whole human race—or would such information be restricted through the patenting mechanism? Mediating these two extremes is a three-fold process articulated by Watson: First, those who develop the information have an opportunity to explore it; second, the information will then be shared with scientists in other countries who have borne their share of the cost and burdens of the research; third, the information would be published and accessible to everyone.[34]

Another issue of justice identified by Lebacqz is what return the taxpayer, who basically funds the HGP, might expect. This is of particular interest since many tax dollars are subsidizing HGP research by private industry. Lebacqz suggests that price controls on pharmaceuticals would not be an unreasonable expectation. Otherwise the taxpayer would pay twice: once through taxes supporting the research, and then for the product itself, especially if it is sold at a monopoly price.[35]

A related issue is the amount of money directed to the HGP at the cost of other research products, particularly in biology. In 1990, Martin Rechsteiner of the University of Utah argued that the genome project is "a waste of national resources."[36] "Between 1988 and 1990, when the genome budget had risen from roughly $17 million to $88 million, the NIGMS [National Institute for General Medical Sciences] budget exclusive of AIDS research had risen from $613 million to only $667 million, an increase that failed even to offset inflation in the cost of biomedical research."[37] Additionally, in 1988 the National Institutes of Health awarded 43 percent fewer grants than it had the previous year.[38] Yet Daniel Kevles and Leroy Hood in their book *The Code of Codes* do not argue that the HGP is the main cause of this funding problem. The politics and administration of NIH are also part of the problem. Furthermore, the number of completed Ph.D.'s has increased dramatically. Kevles and Hood note that "funds for biomedical research will not—because they cannot—increase indefinitely at the disproportionately high rate necessary to accommodate all the new Ph.D.s."[39] Yet many scientists have very different stakes in this funding debate, so while the major funding battle may have been won, skirmishes will continue.

Another dimension is—or will be—the developing gap between diagnosis and therapy, an issue mentioned several times before in this book because of its relevance to many facets of the new genetics. The information emerging daily from the HGP will give us the capacity to identify more and more genes that are singly or in groups responsible for various diseases. Sometimes these genes are the direct cause of the disease, and sometimes they may indicate a predisposition to diseases like cancer, heart disease, or Alzheimer's. The identification of such relations between gene and disease will become easier as the mapping of the genome becomes more developed. What will not become easier is developing cures for such diseases, especially the ones that are caused by multiple genes. The only apparent gains will be an increase in anxiety, increased pressure on decisions related to prenatal diagnosis, and greater frustration about being given knowledge that has no practical resolution in terms of prevention or cures.

The availability of tests, particularly tests for cancer, is causing debate within the genetics community. Dr. Francis Collins, director of the HGP, said: "Unanimously, the professional genetics community, the Human Genome Council, and the National Breast Cancer Coalition have stated that these tests should not now be made available."[40] But others are gearing up to make these tests available to physicians. OncorMed, a biotech company in Maryland, has signed an agreement with an association of cancer specialists to perform a test for them and "has advertised to doctors outside the network that it can now test patients for cancer genes."[41] Barbara Weber, M.D., a breast cancer specialist at the University of Pennsylvania School of Medicine, identified two problems with the test. The first is diagnostic and is related to the large variety of mutations of the gene. The patient may have a mutation not seen before, so its cancer potential would be unknown. "If they do not find any mutations, they still cannot be completely reassuring because the woman may have a mutation in a second, recently discovered breast cancer gene or she may have a mutation in a breast cancer gene that is as yet undiscovered."[42] The second problem relates to the aftermath of the test: "Once we get this information, we are not able to help very much in terms of prevention."[43] Thus the patient is left with bad news and no options, preventive or therapeutic.

The strongest arguments in favor of making such tests available rely on the old ethical warhorse of autonomy. Accordingly, Dr. David Sidransky of Johns Hopkins School of Medicine comments: "It is unethical to prevent patients from having tests for cancer genes if they want them."[44] But the trump card is American pragmatism. Again says Sidransky: "They [patients] will go anywhere, to another country if they have to. There will be clinics set up to do it. Is that going to be better than having it available in the United States?"[45]

But these arguments do not deal with the reliability of the tests, with the usefulness or even appropriateness of the information to be gained, or with what can be offered as therapy, if there is any, to the patient. If such tests are driven by a combination of the market and autonomy, ultimately the patients themselves may lose in the long run. For what they learn might not be beneficial if the outcome is not preventable or if therapy is not available. It is one thing to discover an unexpected illness during the course of an examination and quite another to screen for the susceptibility to illnesses—either prenatally, during childhood, or in early adulthood. More specifically, it is one thing to learn one has cancer and quite another to learn that one is going to contract cancer regardless of what one does to prevent it. Such information may test us in ways we have not thought of before—knowledge may not always be the blessing we think it is.

The information being learned through modern genetics is exciting, important, and controversial. As we progress deeper into the genome with the aid of the map the HGP is developing, new problems and controversies will emerge. What is called for is continued vigilance, continued examination of the issues, and a careful ethical and social evaluation of the projects and their implications. These tasks are not easy, but they are eminently human, particularly since we are, in the words of Teilard de Chardin, "evolution become conscious of itself."

NOTES

1. For a specifically Catholic approach to this issue, see the interesting and helpful article by Carol Tauer, "Preventing the Transmission of Genetic Diseases," *Chicago Studies* 33 (November 1994): 213–27.
2. Nelson A. Wivel and LeRoy Walters, "Germ-Line Gene Modification and Disease Prevention: Some Medical and Ethical Perspectives," *Science* 262 (1993): 533.
3. Ibid.
4. Theodore Friedman, "Progress Toward Human Gene Therapy," *Science* 244: 1275.
5. W. French Anderson, "Human Gene Therapy," *Science* 256 (1992): 812.
6. Ibid.
7. Wivel and Walters, "Germ-Line Gene Modification," 533.
8. Ibid.
9. Anderson, "Human Gene Therapy," 812.
10. Ibid.
11. Ibid.
12. Wivel and Walters, "Germ-Line Gene Modification," 536.
13. Charles C. Mann, "Behavioral Genetics in Transition," *Science* 264 (1994): 1686.
14. Marcia Barinaga, "A New Tool for Examining Multigenic Traits," *Science* 264 (1994): 1691.
15. Mann, "Behavioral Genetics in Transition," 1687.
16. Ibid.
17. Ibid., 1688.
18. Robert Plomin, Michael J. Owen, Peter McGuffin, "The Genetic Basis of Complex Human Behaviors," *Science* 264 (1994): 1736.
19. Jerome Kagan, "The Realistic View of Biology and Behavior," *Chronicle of Higher Education*, 5 October 1994, A64.
20. Quoted in Mann, "Behavioral Genetics in Transition," 1689.
21. Robert Plomin, "The Role of Inheritance in Behavior," *Science* 248: 187.
22. Ibid.
23. Ibid.
24. Robert Wright, "The Biology of Violence," *The New Yorker* 71 (13 March 1995): 71.
25. Ibid.

26. Ibid.
27. Ibid.
28. Ibid.
29. Daniel J. Kevles, "The X Factor," *The New Yorker*, 3 April 1995, 90.
30. Philip Elmer-Dewitt, "Cloning: Where Do We Draw the Line?" *Time*, 8 November 1993, 69.
31. Here I am explicitly using the ethics method of John Duns Scotus, a fuller account of which can be found in *Theological Studies* 53 (June 1993): 272–93.
32. Quoted in Jane Gross, "Thinking Twice About Cloning: Jokes Give Way to Worries," *New York Times* (New England ed.), 27 February 1997, A25.
33. Karen Lebacqz, "Fair Shares: Genes and Justice," in *Genes, Religion, and Society*, ed. Ted Peters (New Haven, CT: Yale University Press, 1996), 5.
34. Ibid., 11.
35. Ibid., 21.
36. Quoted in Daniel J. Kevles and Leroy Hood, "Reflections," in Daniel J. Kevles and Leroy Hood, *The Code of Codes: Scientific and Social Issues in the Human Genome Project* (Cambridge, MA: Harvard University Press, 1992), 300.
37. Ibid., 301.
38. Ibid., 302.
39. Ibid., 303.
40. Quoted in Gina Kolata, "Tests to Assess Risks for Cancer Raising Questions," *New York Times*, 27 March 1995, A1.
41. Ibid., A9.
42. Ibid.
43. Ibid.
44. Ibid.
45. Ibid.

Chapter 9
Nine

CONCLUSION:
METHODOLOGICAL CONSIDERATIONS

GIVEN THE VAST ARRAY of themes identified in the preceding chapters—together with the complex public policy and the ecological and economic issues involved in the debates over the new genetics—coming to conclusions about genetic engineering can be a very difficult project. In part this difficulty is technical in that there is an enormous amount of biological data to collect and understand prior to any decision making. Moreover, reaching conclusions entails making predictions about the consequences and implications, both short-term and long-term, of a particular genetic intervention or use of a genetically engineered product. Then one must examine the policy options and interests of various actors: government, private industry, advocacy groups, and citizens. Finally, one needs to look at the ethical method by which one makes decisions. Material in the previous chapters has looked at various technical, political, and policy issues. To conclude, I will examine some methodological issues of the new genetics.

How one starts the process of ethical decision making reveals much about how one resolves the issues. I want to describe briefly two approaches and suggest why I think one is preferable.

The first approach is called a *deontological* or a *principles approach*. This method of decision making begins with a principle(s) and then applies it to all the cases. Thus one deduces from the principle how a case is to be resolved. For example, John Robertson, in his book *Children of Choice: Freedom and the New Reproductive Technologies*, argues that

> procreative liberty should enjoy presumptive primacy when conflicts about its exercise arise because control over whether one reproduces or not is central to personal identity, to dignity, and to the meaning of one's life. For example, deprivation of the ability to avoid reproduction determines one's self-determination in the most basic sense.[1]

The principle, then, serves as the starting point and touchstone in any and all decision making with respect to reproductive and, by implication, genetic decisions. In essence, this value with its presumptive primacy, even though this is argued for on consequentialist or utilitarian grounds, serves as a trump card over other conflicting values.

Another example of the deontological approach comes from the recent encyclical of Pope John Paul II on bioethical issues, *Evangelium Vitae*. In speaking about various techniques of artificial reproduction, the pope argues that they "actually open the door to new threats against life. Apart from the fact that they are morally unacceptable, since they separate procreation from the fully human context of the conjugal act, these techniques have a high rate of failure."[2] The value of the inseparability of procreation from the act of heterosexual intercourse serves as a moral trump over other competing values, no matter how compelling.

What is interesting to note, of course, is that one derives contradictory conclusions from these two examples. But the critical issue is the starting point, not the consequences; for in neither of these systems do other competing values count as much as does the first principle. Nor do various circumstances or outcomes of the principle count. What is important is the primary principle itself with which one starts. Once one knows this, one can resolve most problems by appeal to this principle.

A second approach to decision making revolves, to varying degrees, around considerations of both the *end result* and the *consequences* of a particular action. In this perspective, what is noteworthy is the development of a conclusion in relation to an evaluation of the purpose of the action and its various outcomes. One example of this type of analysis is traditional utilitarianism. Through this method a conclusion is arrived at by comparing the benefits and the burdens of the possible outcomes of an action. That is, after the benefits and burdens have been delineated, the results are weighed against each other so that the outcome bearing the most net benefit can be chosen. While this procedure does not necessarily rule out a consideration of values or principles, they take a backseat to a consideration of the benefits and burdens of the various outcomes. Discussions about whether or not to carry out various genetic screening programs are frequently cast in these terms: One would consider the cost of the test, the reliability of the test, the number of afflicted people who would be identified, the money saved by early intervention. If the ratio between the money expended to do the screening and the money saved through early intervention is favorable, one could decide to proceed with the program.

Another example of this results-oriented form of decision making is called *proportionalism*. Developed by a number of Roman Catholic moral theologians, this approach, while not ignoring key moral principles, considers the end of the action, the intention of the actor, and the relation between premoral values and disvalues in the act and the moral values and disvalues in the outcome. This approach recognizes that in any act there are any number of such premoral values and disvalues. For example, in surgery, the skin of a person is cut open and bones frequently need to be cut. And chemotherapy has any number of very problematic side effects—loss of hair, loss of appetite, nausea, and so forth. These harms, or premoral disvalues, are not only present in the therapy, but they are inherently bound with it in the contemporary practice of medicine. Such harms are beyond our control and choice. But we also know that surgery or chemotherapy produces other outcomes: health, well-being, and a possible cure. What justifies accepting the presence of the premoral evils attached to these two forms of treatment is the moral value of the cure or the well-being expected from the treatment.

The previous examples showed a premoral evil being outweighed by moral goods to be obtained. But premoral goods can also be subverted by a moral evil. For instance, we know that when we help someone, there is a feeling of personal satisfaction that comes with that. This is present within the act as a premoral value or good. Yet, even though helping someone is a premoral good, doing so to put someone in our debt or to curry favor negates the good in the act and creates a moral evil. Here the premoral good is subverted by our intention, and the resulting act is morally wrong.

These two broadly defined methods of ethical decision making form a general context in which to consider material developed later in this chapter. My own preference is to move in the direction of proportionalism, but with some variations.

Before we advance to a consideration of specific ethical issues to which decision-making approaches can be applied, there are several general considerations that I think are important to evaluate as a way of helping to identify and set out these issues.

1. *On what basis does one propose a genetic intervention?* There are two general answers to this question: One basis is therapeutic and the other is enhancement. Each takes us in a rather different direction.

Generally speaking, therapeutic interventions are initiated to correct a specific disease. The purpose is to cure the disease or, if that is not possible, to restore the patient to the best state of health possible. In interventions of this type there are a set of risks and benefits that are generally known. While at times such therapeutic interventions are experimental, they occur as developments of established procedures and are typically part of a research protocol so that the outcomes can be evaluated. But the key issue in therapy is the intent to *restore* the patient to a state of health or well-being.

If the intent is enhancement, however, one is attempting to go beyond current standards and understandings of health and well-being; one is attempting to augment specific characteristics through active intervention or to give an individual a capacity he or she might not have had before. A current example of enhancement is the use of growth hormones in boys of average or lower than average height to make them taller, with a view toward increasing their social status or making them more desirable athletes. (Whether parents will bring their daughters in for similar treatment in light of the growing interest in women's basketball remains to be seen.) Another candidate for enhancement is intelligence, but thus far there are no clearly effective methods, other than the traditional ones of hard work and study. The list of desired characteristics could be extended indefinitely. What is critical here is the desire to *exceed* the standard, to *enhance* a particular characteristic, or to *add* a brand-new or different characteristic to one's genetic makeup. Presently we do not have, in my judgment, a good set of criteria to evaluate such interventions or to consider their social outcomes.

2. *What are the motives for genetic interventions?* A variety of motives are possible: behavioral, social, medical, political, and economic. Each of these has a number of value implications attached to it, as well as considerable social outcomes. Additionally, many of these motives may be intertwined and difficult to evaluate separately. A screening program, for example, may be initiated for medical reasons, such as the sickle-cell anemia screening program of the mid-1960s. But this program was also perceived to have social implications in that individuals so identified were labeled and stigmatized. Furthermore, political motives were ascribed through allegations of potential genocide because of the implications of the program for abortion. A critical point, then, is to recognize that while a program may be initiated with the best of motives, one must also think critically and imaginatively about its implications and its possible relation to other motives.

3. *Who establishes or validates motives for interventions?* If an intervention is possible and desirable, questions yet remain: For example, Who decides and sets the agenda? A wide variety of candidates are possible: scientists, physicians, politicians, lawyers, citizens, patients or relatives of patients, or various combinations of any of the above.

What is important here is to establish the basis of one's claim of both authority and expertise. The claim to authority may be easier to establish given credentials or a specific social role. The claim to expertise may be more difficult given the frequency of the fallacy of the generalization of expertise. This fallacy assumes that because one is an expert in one area, such expertise extends to all other areas of life. When one claims a right or an entitlement to initiate or implement a program or intervention, serious consideration of qualifications is in order.

4. *What are the risks of intervention?* In traditional medicine we are accustomed to having patients and their families consider the risks of various therapeutic interventions. This is a well-established part of the informed consent process. But when we move from the traditional medical model to that of

genetic engineering—even for a therapeutic intervention—we move into somewhat unknown ground. First, the locus of analysis shifts from the individual to social and possible environmental impacts; this is a critical shift of scale in our considerations. And given the intervention—the use of genetically engineered plants, for example—the environmental impacts may take precedence over more traditional considerations.

For many genetic experiments, we simply have no precedent for evaluation because these experiments are being done literally for the first time. The important issue here is to structure the design of the experiment to proceed as carefully as possible and in a controlled way so that the outcomes can be continually monitored. Also of critical importance is the honest reporting of data. We know that in the last several years there have been numerous accounts of data faking. If there is anything that will discredit the already complex and highly politicized field of genetic engineering, it is such practices as this. Scrupulous honesty and the avoidance of even the suggestion of impropriety in the conduct of research are of the highest priority here.

5. *What are the benefits of interventions and who receives them?* This question is much more complicated than it has been in the past. For openers, we have as actors multinational and international corporations and their stockholders and investors, as well as the individual researchers and the corporations and/or universities of which they are members. Then we have the various dimensions of the patenting debate, which have already been discussed. Clearly, much more money is riding on the new genetics than was the case with traditional biomedical research.

Are the benefits to be achieved from genetic research actual or promised? Are they likely to be achieved in the near future or not? Of significance here is again the potential gap between promise and delivery. As indicated before, much of the genome project was sold to the U.S. government and people on the basis of delivering major health benefits. If the present is a reliable guide, such benefits are part of a distant future. The development of even diagnostic tests is proving difficult enough; therapeutic interventions are at a much more considerable distance.

Also pertinent here is Lebacqz's earlier-cited statement concerning double burden of payment for therapeutic interventions. So the issues of benefit involves a critical socioeconomic dimension that did not previously play a role in the overall picture.

The most critical element in thinking of benefits in this context is the necessity of incorporating the social reception and distribution of benefits. We typically think of benefits in fairly individualistic terms—the patient, or the patient and the physician, or the researcher reaps the reward. Although this traditional way of thinking about benefits includes a social dimension, both the scale and the range of benefits are changed radically by the new presence of the corporate dimension of genetic engineering.

6. *What is our vision of the future?* The new genetics has brought with it new powers, capacities, and abilities. We can intervene in nature in radically new ways, and these can lead to a particular future. But what will this future look like? Who will be the main actors in it? Whose choices and desires will be implemented? What will its politics be? If one turns to science fiction, one typically finds fairly frightening scenarios. If one turns to some religious groups, one finds various apocalyptic and cataclysmic projections. If one turns to some scientists, one finds unbounded confidence and optimism. Reality may turn out to have elements of some or none of these perspectives.

Yet the future is something we must consider. For our contemporary choices are the first dawnings of a future that will be, in profound and unprecedented ways, one of our own choosing.

*   *   *

I would now like to consider several elements that I think are important in coming to a final moral judgment about particular acts of genetic engineering. These considerations emerge from work I have been doing on issues of methodology in ethics, particularly in Scotus's ethics.[3] I used this methodology in evaluating the morality of cloning in the previous chapter and wish to specify it more formally here. The method incorporates a sensitivity to circumstances and outcomes but also takes into account what it is we are doing by considering both the intention of the actor and the object of the act.

Because bioethical problems are interdisciplinary, one needs first to set out the relevant data or material from the appropriate disciplines. The range of disciplines can include, but is not limited to, such fields as science, medicine, law, public health, theology or religious studies, and economics. My point is not that each possible field must be factored into the decision, but that we have to recognize that bioethical decisions, and particularly decisions having to do with genetics, are complex problems. We cannot remain innocent of the various contexts of the problem and assume that we are responsible, ethical decision makers. Thus the very first step in ethical decision making is to define the relevant data from the appropriate disciplines as clearly as one can.

Second, one must identify the relevant values involved in the specific issue. What is at stake in this problem? What are the social, religious, economic, political, and medical values involved and what are some of the implications? Again the issue is the identification of the complexity of the problem and the realization that simple solutions to complex problems usually don't work, precisely because a simple solution cannot capture the nuances of a complex situation.

Third, I think it is important either to be aware of or to explicitly name various organizations and institutions to which any decision maker belongs and to which one owes some loyalty. For once we identify the relevant values and begin to rank them, the question of loyalty becomes important. What we consider most and least important may reflect our own interests and loyalties with respect to our various memberships. While such memberships are not necessarily normative for our decision making, they can and do exert influence on us. We at least need to be aware that we come to a decision with a dynamic complex of interests and loyalties from our associations that provides us with a particular perspective.

With regard to the question of methodology, first we must consider both the intention of the actor and the object of the act. I group these together because I think the intention helps define the object to a large degree. In other words, a specification of what we are doing gives a generic understanding of the morality of the act. But this specification is not enough. This is where the intention becomes a critical moral refinement of the object. That is, I must ask now, What is it that I specifically intend through this particular act in reference to this object? The intention makes more particular the specific moral dimensions of the act by identifying the moral nuances of the various dimensions and implications of the act.

I do not want to argue that the object of the act is irrelevant or totally up to the discretion of the individual; there are premoral values and disvalues that are built into the nature of reality and that must be taken into account. For example, abortion will always involve killing—and that is a significant premoral disvalue. But this determination brings killing into a general moral discussion. Also necessary for a moral judgment is the appropriate description of the act to present its full moral dimensions. Here is where the intention is particularly important, for it initiates that process by specifying what it is one is aiming at in so acting.

Next, in a further specification of the moral dimensions of an action, we need to first consider the circumstances of the act, particularly the circumstances of the end, the way the act is performed, the likely success of the act, and the circumstance of place. (Recall the application of this stage's steps that we conducted in Chapter 8.) Scotus makes an argument about the moral relevance of circumstances. He argues that a name, such as "theft" or "adultery," can be used to signify both an act and its impropriety: The "name 'adultery' signifies not just the natural act of copulation, but also its impropriety in that this act is not done with one's own spouse."[4] He goes on to say that while it would not seem that the sort of acts signified by adultery or theft "could possibly be good, . . . it is possible for the underlying act to exist without the deformity, for instance, the act of intercourse or that of appropriating such a thing."[5] In the specific case of lying, then, what makes it sinful is *both* the utterance of specific words *and* the intention of deceiving. In this case, "in addition to the underlying act there are such circumstances as necessarily deform it."[6] Thus one must look beyond the act itself to the circumstances in which it is performed to understand its moral significance. The intentionality of the agent is again of critical significance here.

Our second consideration is the circumstance of manner; that is, how the act ought to be performed. This again is related to the appropriateness of the act and the way in which the act will enhance the goodness of the agent. This is an important dimension because it recognizes that what we do in turn makes us into particular moral beings. An act is not something external to us; rather, what we do and how we do it shapes and forms us.

The circumstance of appropriate time refers to whether an act can be "directed to or can attain such an end."[7] That is, will the action actually effect the end? To a large degree this looks to the issue of the likelihood of the success of the action. One could also reasonably include in this dimension a consideration of the cost of success. This opens the door to a risk-benefit and benefit-burden analysis in terms of calculating the actual success of the act.

Finally, Scotus notes the circumstance of place, which he does not fully define, and claims that it often plays no part in moral consideration. One can see, though, that an act may have an appropriate end, be done in an appropriate manner and at a suitable time, but might still cause scandal to another. This would render the act morally wrong because of the circumstance of place. Again this opens up the way to a broader social analysis of the act. Does the act uncritically reflect dominant social values? Does it challenge them? Does the act respond to only a narrow constituency?

Scotus concludes that the

> moral goodness of an act is a kind of decor it has, including a combination of due proportion to all to which it should be proportioned (such as the potency, the object, the end, the time, the place, and the manner), and this especially as right reason dictates should pertain to the act, so that we could say of all these things that it is their conformity to right reason that is essential. If this is given, then the act is good, and if this is not given, then—whatever else the act may have—it is not good.[8]

*   *   *

Throughout this book I have considered a number of issues and problems, each with a scientific and ethical dimension. The problems are both thematic, as in the concepts of the sanctity of life and considerations of nature and disease, and specific, as in gene therapy, bioengineered foods, and patenting genetically engineered animals.

Some issues seem to be a little clearer and more susceptible to resolution than others. I would think that gene therapy would be one such case, for it fits within the traditional and well-grounded model of research ethics. That is, we have available a reasonably well-accepted framework for analyzing various aspects of this new development. One aspect is the informed consent process, which ensures that patients have the appropriate level of information with respect to both processes and possible outcomes. The critical issues, because of the novelty of the intervention, will be safety and risk. Not all of the risks may be fully known, and uncertainty has to be factored into the consent process. Offsetting that, however, is the high degree of review and evaluation these protocols for gene therapy receive both on a local and a national level. While there may be disagreement over whether a particular experiment should be done, I think that with a procedure such as this at least the framework of analysis is clear and widely accepted and has a fairly successful history to which we may appeal.

Less clear in their analysis are genetically engineered products such as the FlavrSavr tomato and foods engineered to contain a vaccine. Historically, both plants and animals have been bred and crossbred to produce new and improved foods and animals. We are all familiar with Frank Purdue's claim of how it takes a tough man to produce a tender chicken. So again we have a history within which to begin thinking about this kind of development. Yet the history has a significant limit. Past breeding efforts have been within a species and have been to select for characteristics already present there. Genetic engineering gives us the capacity to take a gene from one species and place it in another and have that organism act in a new way. Thus the antifreeze gene from the Arctic flounder has been placed in some tomatoes to prevent them from freezing. Human growth factor has been placed in pigs to get them to grow bigger faster.

One issue raised by these developments is that of the integrity of species. Another has to do with the health implication, if any, for humans and/or other animals who eat these products. A third problem area is the environmental impact, if any, of these products. Finally, what is the process of FDA review for the new products that do not fit traditional guidelines? Again, while there are some frameworks available for initial evaluation, new approaches must be developed and these may not be easy to generate. The issues are complex and their resolution remains uncertain.

Finally, there are those issues that are not at all clear in terms of analysis or resolution, and these are predictably highly controverted. Such is the issue with which I began this book: the patenting of various life-forms such as transgenic mice, food products, or bacteria. In the Introduction I indicated the spectrum of problems that this issue can raise. Here I wish to focus on the structuring of the debate. The "Joint Appeal Against Human and Animal

Patenting" suggests that such patents and the indiscriminate use of the techniques of genetic engineering threaten the dignity and integrity of human life and that life and its building blocks belong to God, not patent holders. Additionally, the statement makes several claims about what has been done, is being done, and might be done. What is one to make of such claims? This question is particularly important since the statement received widespread media attention and raises critical issues.

First, the statement begs important questions by suggesting that developments and application in genetic engineering are being done indiscriminately: What *is* being done? Is this indiscriminate? And, if so, by what criteria is it deemed so? Second, the statement talks of genetically engineering and patenting human embryos. Though this particular statement is conditioned by the term *can*, which merely suggests capability, the way the sentence is worded gives the impression that these procedures are actually being done. Important questions here are: Is this the case? And, if so, what do these terms mean? Third, and most important, the statement claims that a California company has been granted commercial ownership of human bone marrow "stem cells" and that such a patent had never before been allowed on an unaltered human body part. Is this claim accurate? Two colleagues of mine at the Center for Theology and the Natural Sciences in Berkeley telephoned SyStemix, the company that was not named in the statement but that holds the patent. Unfortunately for the statement, the patent does not cover stem cells, or an unaltered body part, or anything in the body of the person.

I do not want to argue here that the religious leaders intentionally misled anyone. They themselves may have been misled, they may have misunderstood the facts, or they may have misrepresented what they wanted to say. But I do want to argue that this statement has done a tremendous disservice to the general public and to the scientific community because it makes a claim that is simply not true. The consequence is that the broader areas of legitimate concern and debate are now dismissible because they too have been painted with the brush of a lie, a misrepresentation, or a philosophy that argues that the end justifies the means. Religious concerns have been made to look foolish and religious leaders appear incompetent. So the context for a legitimate and rigorous debate of the issues has now been poisoned.

I raise these three concerns with this statement to argue that even if there is broad agreement over some of the terms of the genetic debate, there are significant problems that remain. The methodological elements I have presented in this chapter are neither a definitive account of moral reasoning nor a fail-safe way to make ethical decisions. What I do think they provide is a way of ensuring that critical pieces of the ethical agenda are included in a consistent and coherent way. The decision-making process in thinking through ethical problems in genetics and genetic engineering is extremely complex.

My hope is that this proposal is helpful in working through the complex and difficult personal and social agendas of resolving ethical issues in the new genetics.

NOTES

1. John Robertson, *Children of Choice: Freedom and the New Reproductive Technologies* (Princeton, NJ: Princeton University Press, 1995), 24.
2. Pope John Paul II, *Evangelium Vitae*, in *The Encyclicals of John Paul II* J. Michael Miller, C.S.B. ed. (Huntington, IN: Our Sunday Visitor Publishing Division, 1996), Para. 14, 803.
3. Here I will explicitly use the ethics method of John Duns Scotus, a fuller account of which can be found in my work in either *Theological Studies* 53 (June 1993): 272–93, or *The Ethical Theory of John Duns Scotus* (Quincy, IL: Franciscan University Press, 1995).
4. *Ordinatio* III, suppl. dist. 38, art. 2; quoted in Allan B. Wolter, O.F.M., *Duns Scotus on the Will and Morality* (Washington, DC: Catholic University of America Press, 1986), 487.
5. *Ordinatio* III, suppl. dist. 38, art. 2; quoted in ibid.
6. Ibid.
7. *Quodlibet*, q. 18; quoted in ibid., 217.
8. *Ordinatio* I, dist. 17, n. 62; English translation by Allen B. Wolter, O.F.M., *Pro manuscripto*, 207.

INDEX

133